T0305858

The Problem-Solving, Problem-Prevention, and Decision-Making Guide

Organized and Systematic
Roadmaps for Managers

The Problem-Solving, Problem-Prevention, and Decision-Making Guide

Organized and Systematic Roadmaps for Managers

Bob Sproull

CRC Press
Taylor & Francis Group
Boca Raton London New York

CRC Press is an imprint of the
Taylor & Francis Group, an **informa** business
A PRODUCTIVITY PRESS BOOK

CRC Press
Taylor & Francis Group
6000 Broken Sound Parkway NW, Suite 300
Boca Raton, FL 33487-2742

© 2018 by Taylor & Francis Group, LLC
CRC Press is an imprint of Taylor & Francis Group, an Informa business

No claim to original U.S. Government works

ISBN 13: 978-0-8153-6140-4 (hbk)

Library of Congress Cataloging in Publication Data

Names: Sproull, Robert, author.
Title: The problem-solving, problem-prevention, and decision-making guide :
organized and systematic roadmaps for managers / Bob Sproull.
Description: New York : Taylor & Francis, [2018] | Includes bibliographical references
and index.
Identifiers: LCCN 2017054324 (print) | LCCN 2018007385 (ebook) |
ISBN 9781351116268 (eBook) | ISBN 9780815361404 (hardback : alk. paper)
Subjects: LCSH: Decision making. | Problem solving. | Industrial management.
Classification: LCC HD30.23 (ebook) | LCC HD30.23 .S7216 2018 (print) |
DDC 658.4/03--dc23
LC record available at https://lccn.loc.gov/2017054324

Visit the Taylor & Francis Web site at
http://www.taylorandfrancis.com

and the CRC Press Web site at
http://www.crcpress.com

Contents

Preface

When I was a much, much younger man, just starting my manufacturing career at Xerox Corporation, I remember how one day my new boss called me into his office and told me that he had a problem he wanted me to solve for him. Since it was my first real assignment of substance, I was anxious and wanted to impress him by doing a great job. The only problem was I had no idea how to begin to solve problems and, quite frankly, I was too embarrassed to ask for help. After all, it's what he hired me to do, so I frantically searched the library (in those days there was no Internet to surf for answers) for a simple reference book on problem solving to guide me, but I couldn't find one. I couldn't sleep and I spent days and nights worrying about what to do. I finally did solve the problem, but only after weeks and weeks of simple trial and error, trying different things until I just happened onto the solution. I had no real approach, just simple logic on what I should do next. I realized then that there was a critical need for something to lead or guide people like me through a problem-solving exercise.

It seems that since that day forty-plus years ago not much has changed. I've met lots of people working on problems and lots of people complaining about problems, but very few who actually understand how to systematically search for and find the root causes of problems. Just like myself as a young man, many people don't even know where or how to begin to solve a problem. We humans tend to get bogged down in the minutiae of the unimportant details and fail to realize that solving problems really isn't that difficult if we simply follow an organized, disciplined, and systematic approach.

I also see many people making bad decisions, jumping to conclusions, or simply treating the symptoms of problems rather than solving them. Every day we are confronted with a plethora of real problems and decisions. Problems that are creating issues like lost throughput, poor quality, personnel problems, and material shortages, and decisions that must be made correctly and efficiently. How we approach these daily quandaries will determine how successful we are at resolving problems and making good decisions. It has been my experience that people like to jump directly into causes and solutions before they even understand the nature of the problem they are trying to solve. Likewise, making good decisions comes only after weeks of effort. As a result, they end up making blind decisions that change perfectly acceptable processes for all the wrong reasons. The danger in this type of approach is that it typically adds numerous non-value-added process steps that complicate, create waste, and destabilize the processes and systems. It is this waste of time, waste of motion, and waste of materials that drive many companies to financial ruin or, worse yet, closure.

The real secret to solving problems does not depend upon the number of sophisticated statistical tools that you know how to use. As a matter of fact, the secret to solving most problems is to keep your approach simple and uncomplicated. Where many people go wrong is that they fail to do what Toyota does so effortlessly. They fail to "go and see." Solving problems starts by simply going to the problem, observing it, and fully understanding it. As you will see in the chapters that follow, by following a structured approach and using only simple tools, most problems will be solved. And the same can be said for making effective decisions and preventing problems.

The cornerstones of this book are three roadmaps for *solving problems, preventing problems*, and *making decisions*. Each roadmap contains a step-by-step explanation on how to solve existing problems, how to prevent future problems, and how to make effective decisions. I also devote much of this book to real case studies for each of the techniques presented.

This book also contains the four basic tools that I have successfully used to solve most problems I have encountered during my career. It is my belief that if you can master the use of these four basic tools, "go and see" the problem, and use my roadmaps to guide you, that you will become much better at solving problems, preventing problems, and making good decisions. I have witnessed many very ordinary people deliver very extraordinary results by simply following the structured roadmaps presented in this book. Solving and preventing problems, and making effective decisions does not have to be full of stress and anxiety if you will simply follow my roadmaps.

Good luck! But remember, my definition of luck is laboring under correct knowledge. That is, you make your own luck!

1

The DNA of Problems and Problem Solvers

Problems do not go away. They must be worked through or else they remain, forever a barrier to the growth and development of the spirit.

Scott Peck

1.1 THE DNA OF A GOOD PROBLEM SOLVER

It is my belief that the truly good problem solvers in the world all share a special bond, a connection if you will, and this connection is not coincidental. It is because of specific behaviors and character traits that problem solvers all seem to share. I am convinced it is these traits and behaviors that separate true problem solvers from problem solving wannabes or could-bes. If you've ever worked for Toyota or have been a supplier to Toyota, then you will recognize these traits and behaviors easily. Why Toyota? Because Toyota is the best possible example of a company that truly gets it as it applies to their approach to business in general and, more specifically, problem solving and prevention.

I've cataloged ten behaviors and personality traits that I believe are the basic genetic material shared and utilized by effective problem solvers. I also believe that if a person or team can demonstrate and exploit these behaviors, then the opportunity to become effective and successful at problem solving will materialize. Each of these behaviors and traits, although not listed in order of importance, serve a different purpose or function as the individual or team searches for the answer to the problem-solving conundrum.

1. Being objective
2. Being analytical
3. Being creative
4. Having dedication, commitment, and perseverance
5. Being curious
6. Having courage
7. Having a sense of adventure
8. Being enthusiastic
9. Being patient
10. Being vigilant

Let's look at each of these more closely.

A problem solver must always be *impartial and objective*, and not have preconceived notions, ideas, or biases on what is causing the problem. Each problem has its own set of conditions or circumstances and most of the time the answer lies in the data and information surrounding these conditions. Without objectivity, crucial observations might be ignored or missed. I have witnessed so many times individuals and teams jumping to causes and solutions before even understanding the problem. Keeping an open mind throughout the process is critical.

A good problem solver must be *analytical* and *systematic* in his or her approach to problems. One of the keys to solving problems is the art of asking the right questions in a methodical fashion. As we investigate problems, it is crucial to use a logical approach as we move through the maze of unknown facts and forever-present opinions of others. Asking questions, or should I say the right questions, is imperative if we are to uncover the facts relative to the problem. Closely related to this is the need for analysis. Once the information and data surrounding the problem are collected, they must be analyzed in a systematic way. A good problem solver knows and understands which tools and techniques are available, how to use them, and when to utilize each one.

Solving problems requires *imagination, creativity*, and *ingenuity*. Solving problems sometimes requires abstract thinking, and necessitates imaginative and inventive actions. Once you have determined the true root cause (or causes) of the problem, it's time to be innovative and let your creative juices flow as you develop effective solutions. The solution to your problem will demand ingenuity and resourcefulness, so you must be inventive.

Solving problems requires *dedication, perseverance,* and *commitment,* because the answers are sometimes obscure or concealed and, therefore, not always obvious. One must be determined to find the root cause and committed to using a systematic approach. Good problem solvers don't vacillate as the problem-solving journey unfolds; they stay the course.

A good problem solver has *curiosity.* When people are curious, they are interested in understanding why things happen and will probe below the surface of the problem looking for things that may not be obvious or evident above the surface. Solutions to problems all begin out of the curiosity and desire to determine and understand what happened and then understand why. Until you understand why the problem has emerged, your chances of solving it are pretty much nil.

It takes *courage, daring,* and *guts* to be a good problem solver. Because there is usually always a negative aura or atmosphere surrounding problems, people who are closest to and responsible for the area with the problem sometimes feel threatened. Because they are feeling vulnerable and exposed, they generally don't like to be questioned, but they must have the courage and fortitude to push forward and seek answers. When you ask people questions about the problem in their area of responsibility, many times the instinctive reaction is to take a defensive posture. You are typically perceived as prying and impugning their character. Of course, this isn't really the case, and if you ask the questions in a positive and nonthreatening way, you can ease some of this perception.

Solving problems is a journey and an exploration into what happened, so having a *sense of adventure* is fundamental to reaching your destination. I have often wondered how the early explorers like Columbus or Lewis and Clark must have felt as they sailed into unknown and uncharted waters or passed through unfamiliar and strange countryside, never knowing what they were going to encounter or be confronted with or even if they would be successful. The one thing Toyota does better than any company I have ever seen is its mandate and directive to employees to go visit the source of the problem so they can see firsthand what is happening.

A good problem solver must demonstrate *enthusiasm* during the problem-solving journey. There must be a certain zest, zeal, and passion that becomes contagious and infectious to the rest of the team. By demonstrating and communicating enthusiasm to the team, you are inadvertently motivating and inspiring your team members. There will be times when the situation may appear hopeless to the team, but your positive outlook and enthusiasm will guide you and your team through the process.

Finding root causes and developing solutions to problems are not always clear-cut, straightforward, or uncomplicated, so a good problem solver must demonstrate *patience, persistence,* and *staying power.* You will, at times, be pressured to move faster than you would like to or need to, so you must be compelled to stay the course. Part of learning to be a good problem solver is learning how to become disciplined and regimented. If you take your time and systematically work through problems, your success rate will dramatically improve. Remember, *patience* truly is a virtue.

Finally, a good problem solver should be *vigilant* and always expect the unexpected. Just when you think you may have exposed the root cause of a problem, or have discovered the causal pathway of the problem, new information or something unanticipated may come out of the blue and catch you off guard if you aren't alert to this possibility. So be cautious and attentive that new information could come at any time that will change your point of view.

These are the qualities and behaviors of a good problem solver, but not all of them are necessarily essential in one person for successfully solving a problem. As a matter of fact, it's probably true that if the team possesses these qualities or behaviors as a group, success will follow. If one person is, for example, analytical, curious, patient, and dedicated, while someone else is objective and enthusiastic, and still another has courage and a sense of adventure but is vigilant, then the team holistically satisfies these requisites. It sometimes takes a village to solve problems, so select your team members with these qualities in mind.

1.2 THE PROBLEM WITH PROBLEMS

Problems exist everywhere and we all know when we have one because we can feel and experience their chilling and unsettling presence if they are unpleasant or serious enough. We feel and experience the pressure, demands, and stress to fix them, and if we're not prepared or if we don't know how to begin to solve them, it is not a good feeling at all. Maybe we're getting pressure from the boss who tells us to do something and do it quickly! Maybe the board of directors wants to know what's happened to profit margins or maybe we're getting e-mails or telephone calls from irate, infuriated customers about quality problems or late orders. Whatever the motivation, the normal response to this pressure, for many of us, is that we start making changes and hope for the best!

It's not unusual, for many of us, to make blind adjustments to otherwise stable processes or systems without understanding the simple cause-and-effect relationships that are driving the negative performance. The bottom line is that, characteristically, many of us tend to panic and do stupid things, foolish things, irresponsible things that we might not do if we thought through the problem more or didn't have all this pressure! Whatever the reason or motivation, it is clear that, making pointless or unwarranted changes without understanding why is the worst reaction possible, because it simply complicates and confuses the situation. *That's the problem with problems*: They have a tendency to change our behaviors and make us do things that we instinctively know are wrong. It's almost as if there is some supernatural or paranormal power at work here. To complicate matters, there are different types of problems and each requires a different tactic if we are to resolve them effectively.

1.3 THE DNA OF PROBLEMS

Not all problems are created equal. That may seem intuitive or obvious to you, but it really isn't. When I say that not all problems are created equal, I'm not referring to the basic problem itself, but rather the framework or structure of the problem. There are different categories or types of problems, and it is enormously important that you recognize and distinguish what type of problem you are working on because the approach to one type of problem may not work for another type. Problems are divided into three fundamental categories as follows:

1. Problems that have resulted from a *change* or adjustment from existing conditions, or *change-related* problems.
2. Problems that are persistent and have seemingly been around forever and are therefore *chronic* problems.
3. Problems that are both chronic and change related, or what I call *hybrid* problems.

Now let's take a little closer look at all three problem types.

1.4 CHANGE-RELATED PROBLEMS

I mentioned earlier that problems tend to make us panic and make unwarranted changes, so if these are not the behaviors we should be demonstrating, then what are the right behaviors? Before we answer this, let's review the basic concept of what a problem is. Kepner and Tregoe, in their problem-solving classic *The New Rational Manager*, characterize problems simply as deviations from expected performance [1], but let's look at this more closely. Kepner and Tregoe tell us that a performance standard is achieved when all of the conditions required for acceptable performance are operating as they *should*. This includes everything in our work environment, that is, people, materials, systems, processes, departments, pieces of equipment, and so on—basically everything. Kepner and Tregoe further tell us that "if there is an alteration in one or more of these conditions, that is, if some kind of change occurs, then it is possible that performance will alter too." If performance goes from good to bad or positive to negative, then we feel the pressure. The more serious the effect in the decline in performance, the more pressure there is to find a cause and correct it.

Changes happen every day in our lives so the question becomes, when is the deviation that we observe considered to be a problem? It has been my experience (and that of Kepner and Tregoe) that in order for a deviation to be considered a problem, one or more of the following requirements must be satisfied:

1. The deviation or performance shift must be recognized and perceived as being negative to the organization. That is, the deviation must result in a negative effect to things like a loss in throughput, a deterioration of quality, or a safety performance issue that translates directly into something like a missed delivery to a customer, a loss in revenue or margin erosion, a customer complaint, or an injury.

2. The cause of the performance deviation isn't known. That is, the root cause is not immediately established using "normal" problem-solving techniques, which results in an extended period of time at the new negative performance level. Obviously, if the cause isn't known, then the solution won't be known either, so the performance problem lingers.

3. Both the root cause and the solution are known, but the solution can't be implemented because it either costs too much or takes too

long. As pressure mounts to have the problem fixed, more often than not the symptoms get treated and a quick fix is implemented. This, in turn, usually prolongs the problem episode, or sets the stage for it to return or actually deteriorate even further.

If the root cause and the solution are known and implementing it doesn't take too long and/or cost too much, then the deviation is not deemed to be a problem because it simply gets fixed. In effect, it has no visibility within the organization, at least not in the upper echelon. But when you add the critical factors of cost, time, lost revenues, and so forth, deviations will most likely be portrayed and characterized as problems.

Let's look at an example of a change-related problem. Suppose you are the plant manager of a company that manufactures electronic equipment for the automobile industry. Your plant's budgeted EBITDA% (earnings before income, taxes, depreciation and amortization) is tied to sales revenue and is variable, but has been averaging roughly 25% per month throughout the year. This means that if your annual sales are in the $100 million range, then the annual earnings are expected to be in the neighborhood of $25 million for the year. You've worked hard and you've pretty much hit budget in each of the first five months of the year. The board is pleased with the job you're doing, and you are feeling good about how well your plant is performing. In July, you get a frenzied call from your accountant telling you that the numbers are in for June and they don't look good at all. You tell him to come to your office with the numbers and you both assess the results. Figure 1.1 is the monthly EBITDA% graph and one look at it tells you that your accountant is right. What had been a picture of steady and stable, on-budget earnings from January through May, has

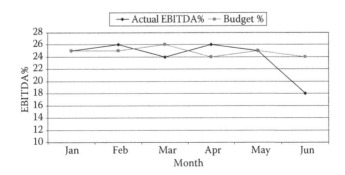

FIGURE 1.1
Monthly EBITDA% versus budget.

abruptly and unexpectedly gone awry by taking a nosedive. You ask your accountant what happened, but he has no idea. A sense of fear, apprehension, and, yes, panic comes over you because you know that this very afternoon the board of directors is coming for its monthly review of your plant's performance. You tell your accountant that you need answers and that you need them right now! The accounting manager leaves and you sit there and rack your brain trying to understand what has happened. You know instinctively that something has changed, but what was it? You think to yourself, "EBITDA% was right on target through May, but in June, it dropped from 25% to 18%." Because the drop in performance was sudden and unexpected, you know you have to find out what *changed*. That's the problem with change-related problems; they are many times unpredictable, sudden, and unexpected. And when the direction of change is toward the negative side of the ledger, many times they cause people to panic.

But sometimes conditions improve and positive changes occur and things go better than expected. But when performance rises or improves unexpectedly, it clearly does not trigger the same urgent response as the negative shift does. What if the reverse had been true for our plant manager? What if his EBITDA% had suddenly improved, as in Figure 1.2? Would the sense of urgency or panic have gripped him as when the EBITDA% had declined? Obviously, it wouldn't have, would it? Why do you suppose this is true? It is because, reason number one, the negative recognition and perception requirement of a problem trumps both of the other reasons.

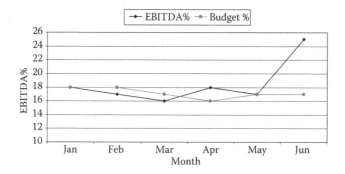

FIGURE 1.2
Monthly EBITDA% versus budget.

Since the plant manager would have known that the board would have been happy with the new EBITDA%, there would have been no negative feelings expressed by the board, and, therefore, little if any pressure to even find out why the positive deviation had occurred.

But beware, do not ignore or disregard positive deviations! Why? Because in my opinion, unexplained positive changes in performance have potentially the same consequences as negative changes. That is, if we don't understand what prompted the positive change in performance, then we certainly won't be able to understand or explain why the performance suddenly changed back to its original, "normal" level of performance, and *it will happen at some point in the future.* The "positive" performance level that had resulted from the original shift in performance will now become the new expected level of performance. So, when the performance metric shifts again to the performance from January through May, it then satisfies the first two requirements of a problem and, therefore becomes classified as a problem. For this reason, it is essential to investigate positive deviations and uncover the root cause or causes.

Because these type problems are always the result of a change, I refer to them as change-related problems. Performance is at a certain level and then a change occurs somewhere in the process resulting in a new performance level. When trying to recognize, understand, and solve problems of this nature, the focus must always be on determining what changed and when it changed. And when you do find the change, the solution usually is simply to reverse the change.

Before leaving our discussion of change-related problems, I need to say something about the change process itself. In many companies I have consulted for, there was no mechanism or system in place to routinely capture process or system changes. Changes happen every day in most businesses and, for the most part, the changes are a good thing, provided they are made under control. (By under control I mean that the change was well conceived, analyzed for potential problems, and, equally important, fully documented.) Documentation of changes becomes critical when problems of this nature are encountered. The documentation should include the specifics of the change and the timing of the change. At the very least, the date should be documented, but if you can record more specific time information like serial numbers or bar code numbers, then problems can be correlated directly to the change.

1.5 CHRONIC PROBLEMS

There is another type of problem that is not necessarily the result of a change, but rather a problem that has been around seemingly forever. Many times, when you ask someone how long this problem has existed, you get a response like "We've always had this defect!" or "This machine has never produced what the others have." I have named this kind of problem a chronic problem, and for those of you that have ever been involved with the Fords or GMs or Chryslers of the world, you will recognize it immediately. Kepner and Tregoe refer to this kind of problem as *day-one problems* [1].

As the name implies, it's the kind of problem that has been around since day one. Maybe it's the launch of a new machine that is supposed to be identical to one or more already in place. But, since the start-up, it has never performed quite like the others. Or maybe the supplier of a raw material has two factories, and product received from one factory has outperformed the other factory from the first delivery of the product. Figure 1.3 is a common example for this type of problem.

In this type of problem there is still the expected level of performance (machine target) of the new machine compared with the actual performance of the other machines making the same or similar product. The deviation is the output between the lower performing machine and the other two, supposedly identical machines. The same rules for deciding whether a problem is a problem apply here, as well as the problem-solving tools and techniques.

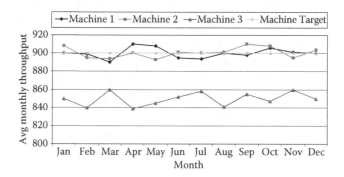

FIGURE 1.3
Average monthly machine throughput versus target.

The major difference between change-related problems and chronic problems is where we focus our efforts. In change-related problems, we focus most of our efforts on determining what changed to create the new level of performance and when the change occurred. But, when we have a situation where the performance of one item has never been what it "should" be compared to one that performs to expectations, we can assume that one of the conditions necessary to attain the expected level of performance does not exist and never has. In this case, we must focus most of our efforts in the area of distinctions, or differences between where or when we have the performance problem compared to where or when we don't. That is, there is something distinct or different when comparing the supposedly identical units, processes, or materials. If we are to successfully solve chronic type problems, then we must find the critical differences or distinctions between the two objects, and take actions that are specifically aimed at eliminating or reducing the differences.

1.6 HYBRID PROBLEMS

Now that we understand the differences between a change-related problem and the chronic problem, you might wonder if it's possible to have both types of problems acting together simultaneously. The answer is an emphatic and categorical yes! When you have an expected level of performance that has never been achieved and it suddenly worsens, you are in the midst of a hybrid problem.

Consider the situation in Figure 1.4. Here we see actual EBITDA% by month, compared to budgeted EBITDA%. The actual EBITDA% has been below budget by approximately 2.5% for the first seven months of the year. In August, the situation worsens, and the gap between expected performance (i.e., EBITDA%) and actual performance grows to about 8%. A situation that I'm sure was filled with pressure and negative energy just became worse.

If you were the owner of these dreadful and deplorable financials, imagine how you would feel and what your actions might be. You have two competing priorities here. On the one hand, you must determine what changed to make the already dismal situation deteriorate, while on the other you must close the gap to the budget. You are in the midst of a hybrid problem, with each part of it competing against the other. The logical

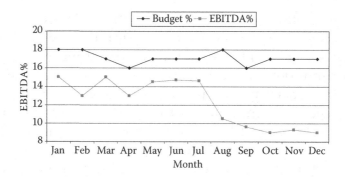

FIGURE 1.4
Monthly EBITDA% versus budget.

approach would be to return to ground zero by finding the change that caused the performance shift, reverse it if possible, and then develop a plan to improve the EBITDA%.

Both are serious problems: One is short term and requires immediate attention, while the other is chronic and requires thoughtful and considerate action! One thing to remember when you are faced with a hybrid problem is to separate the problem into its constituent parts. Disconnect the change-related problem from the chronic problem, because the solution to each will be different.

1.7 THE 4 C'S OF PROBLEM SOLVING

No matter what type of problem you are faced with, there is usually always pressure and anxiety associated with it. You have demands placed on you that can be overwhelming at times. You must take action and implement countermeasures, but that doesn't preclude you from following some sort of logical process. You must remain calm and composed, and sometimes that is difficult to do in the face of a crisis. Most of the time, the immediate actions you take after the problem surfaces are crucial. It is important to realize that the basic actions we take in the face of all problems follow the same logical cycle or sequence of *contain, cause, correct,* and *control*. Each step in this sequence requires your immediate and urgent attention as follows:

1. *Contain the problem*—No matter whether the problem is located within your plant or facility, or has already reached your customer, the first action is to always contain or confine the problem. That is, you must stop the bleeding immediately and limit its scope. If the problem is defective product, you must not permit it to enter the value stream of good product. It is always good practice to physically isolate the problem if there is product involved. If the problem involves people, such as a labor unrest, you must defuse it quickly so it doesn't grow to unmanageable levels.

2. *Find the cause of the problem*—Once you have caged and confined the problem, it is imperative that you find the root cause or origin of the problem. Systematically define and analyze it, and search for the cause or causes. If it is a quality problem, for example, you must find the source of the problem or change that has occurred. If it's a people problem, you must understand what caused the unrest to surface.

3. *Correct the problem*—As soon as the cause of the problem has been determined, you must take swift and pragmatic action to find an effective countermeasure and implement it with expediency. Make certain that you don't just start making changes without justification or reason. Oftentimes you will have options with one solution being short term and the other more long term. What you must decide is how soon the solution must be implemented, and it could be that you find yourself implementing a temporary, short-term solution just to get out of the crisis. It is OK to do this as long as your intention is to implement the longer-term solution later.

4. *Control the problem*—Once the problem has been resolved, always implement some kind of control that will prevent the problem from recurring. When problems persist and recur at customer locations, your credibility takes a hit, so avoid this by implementing a control.

Remaining calm in the face of problems is imperative, so if you will just stop to remember these four actions, you can transform a stressful and taxing situation into one of relative calm and tranquility. In the face of pressure, clearheaded thinking and practical actions are crucial, so simply remember the 4 C's—contain, cause, correct, and control—and you will be in control of the situation.

2

Four Basic Tools for Problem Solving

When the only tool you own is a hammer, every problem begins to resemble a nail.

Abraham Maslow

In my travels, one thing that has become very apparent and evident to me is that there are so many people who have no grasp of basic analysis tools and techniques. One of the prerequisites for solving problems is having at least a basic understanding of which tools to use and when to use them. It is remarkable to me that even after all of the many initiatives and programs like Total Quality Management (TQM) and Six Sigma, so many people and companies haven't embraced or begun to understand the basic tools and concepts. In this chapter, we will consider four basic tools that a problem-solving team must make use of if the team is to successfully determine the root cause of the problem it is addressing. You may be wondering if there are other tools available besides these four, and the answer is yes. But having said this, it is my belief that if you can master and make use of these four simple and uncomplicated tools, then you will be able to solve the majority of problems facing you.

The four tools are the run chart, the Pareto chart, the cause-and-effect diagram, and the causal chain. The *run chart* will answer the questions of when the problem started and when it has occurred since it started, and will then help identify whether it is a change- or launch-related problem. The *Pareto chart* will help the team determine things like where the problem is, which machine is creating the problem, and who has the problem. The *cause-and-effect diagram* will be facilitated with the creation of a list of potential causes, whereas the *causal chain* will help with the team formulate the chain of events that led to the problem (i.e., the hypothesis). Although there are other tools that can be used by the team, I firmly believe that teams will be much more successful by using just these four simple tools. Now let's look at each tool and some examples.

2.1 RUN CHART

One of the keys to solving problems is knowing when the problem began and when it has occurred since its inception. In addition, the team needs to be able to measure the impact of any changes made to the process. The run chart will provide the answer to all of these questions. The run chart or trend chart, as it is also termed, is a graphical representation of the problem being tracked as a function of time, with time being any unit (e.g., hours, days). Time is placed along the horizontal axis (x-axis), and whatever you are measuring is placed along the vertical axis (y-axis). Let's look at an example. Suppose we suspect that temperature is a key factor in the creation of a defect, and we are interested in knowing what happens to the temperature throughout the day. We measure the temperature each hour and record it as follows:

Time	Temperature
6:00 am	60
7:00 am	62
8:00 am	63
9:00 am	65
10:00 am	70
11:00 am	75
12:00 pm	80
1:00 pm	81
2:00 pm	82
3:00 pm	80
4:00 pm	79
5:00 pm	75
6:00 pm	72

Although we are able to view the temperatures as recorded above, and see the general trend, it is sometimes difficult to see other subtleties of how the data is trending, so creating a run chart facilitates this.

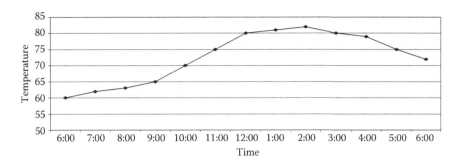

FIGURE 2.1
Temperature versus time of day.

Figure 2.1 is the run chart made from the data collected on temperature every hour. As you can see, the time the temperature was taken is represented along the x-axis, and the actual temperature reading is along the y-axis. From the run chart, we can see that the highest rate of temperature change happens between 9:00 am and 12:00 noon, and that the maximum temperature occurs at 2:00 pm before it begins dropping. The run chart allows us to see exactly what is happening to temperature as a function of time of day. From a problem-solving perspective, if you now record any changes you make directly onto the run chart, the effect is seen immediately. Let's look at a real example.

I have used run charts to solve a variety of problems over the years, but one problem in general stands out as being one of the most distinctive. (Note: This case study will be covered in detail later in Chapter 20.) This problem concerned an engineering group for a company that produced truck bodies for vehicles like moving vans, refrigerated trucks, and landscaping trucks. As the company received orders from customers, it routed the orders through its engineering group, where a cost quote and a build package were prepared. Historically, the normal backlog of orders in engineering was in the 200- to 400-hour range. The actual time required to prepare the quote was about two days, but because there was a backlog of orders waiting to be quoted, the actual time to quote the order and communicate it back to the prospective customer was approximately one week. This amount of time was acceptable to most customers, so there was no problem.

In early 1999 the backlog had grown from the normal 300 hours to over 1500 hours and, as a result, potential customers were unhappy, because the new lead time had grown from seven days to almost forty days. The impact of this increased lead time was that new sales were dropping rapidly and margins were being negatively affected. Customers just didn't want to wait forty days to receive a quote, and this was now recognized as being a significant problem.

In a move designed to reduce the backlog, the vice president of engineering ordered all of his engineers to work overtime until this backlog was reduced. The overtime worked and the backlog was reduced, but several months later, due to the cost of this overtime, the VP was told to stop the overtime. Once again, the backlog grew to over 1200 hours and the VP was relieved of his position and I was called in to fix this problem. This was obviously an example of someone treating the symptoms rather than finding and eliminating the root cause of the problem.

Since the VP left rather abruptly, I had no communication overlap with him and had to rely on any existing data and discussions with the engineers to attempt to understand what was happening. The first thing I did was create a multiyear run chart to get a mental and visual image of what was going on (see Figure 2.2). Once I saw the data plotted in a run chart, I knew two important things. One, the problem we were experiencing was a relatively new problem and, two, whatever changed to cause the increase in backlog hours had occurred somewhere around February 1999. I knew that if I could determine what had changed in the February 1999 time frame, then I had a good chance at solving this problem. Herein lies the true problem-solving value of run charts. By observing the level of the response variable (e.g., backlog hours) as a function of time (months), I could see immediately that the problem was the result of some kind of change and approximately when the change had been made. This is extremely important, because if we can find what changed and reverse it, the response variable should return to its previous acceptable level of

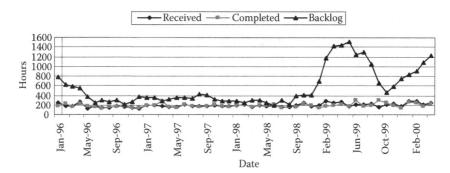

FIGURE 2.2
Engineering backlog, January 1996 to February 2000.

performance. I knew this is what had to be done, so I set in motion a series of interviews with engineers that I knew had been employed during the time frame. I discovered that in December 1998, the former VP had totally reorganized the engineering department into three different areas, depending upon the type of truck body required. In addition, he had also changed how orders were received into engineering at the end of January 1999. Instead of having orders go into a central receptacle within engineering, and then distributing the order to the next available engineer, the new method called for the order quote to go into a receptacle within each of the three groups within engineering. The engineers told me that they had warned the VP that a backlog would probably occur, because he had staffed all three groups equally, even though the percentage of orders for each body type was significantly different and seasonal. The engineers' concerns had been discounted and the backlog began growing.

I immediately returned to the former organizational structure and system of receiving orders, and the backlog decreased nearly as fast as it had increased. In Figure 2.3 you can see that not only did the backlog hours decrease but actually dipped below the level they had been for the previous three years. Because the lead time on new orders through engineering decreased from 40 days to 72 hours and then to 48 hours in 3 months, the market response was a dramatic increase in sales. This simple run chart had identified when the problem had begun, and the effects of the changes we had made to set the stage for one of the most dramatic improvements I have ever been a part of witnessing.

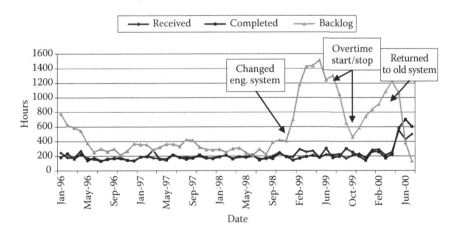

FIGURE 2.3
Engineering backlog, January 1996 to June 2000.

Before we leave our discussion on run charts, I want to reinforce a point I made earlier on how to effectively use a run chart. Although the run chart of the engineering backlog hours looked into the past to help identify what changes had occurred and when the changes were made, it can also be used in reverse. That is, the run chart should be used to evaluate the results of an intended change when implementing a solution to a problem. When the organizational change was made and because of the manner in which the engineering group received incoming orders (Figure 2.3), the backlog began to increase. We labeled the run chart as to what had changed and when the change was made, making it very easy to see the cause-and-effect relationship. In addition, by labeling the chart with when overtime began and ended, we were able to see its short-term effect. Finally, when we implemented our solution (i.e., returning to the original system of handling new orders in engineering), we saw its impact immediately. My point is this: When the team makes changes, record them directly onto the run chart to confirm the impact of your changes and improvements.

2.2 THE PARETO CHART

Whereas the run chart answers the questions of if and when a change has occurred, the Pareto chart is more of a comparative tool. That is, if we suspect differences in performance between things like machines, people, or even days of the week, then we can visualize these differences with a Pareto chart. The genesis of Pareto charts came from a most unlikely source. An Italian economist, Vilfredo Pareto, was studying the distribution of wealth in Italy in the nineteenth century. When he assembled his data, he discovered that approximately 80% of the wealth in Italy was controlled by only 20% of the population. Later Dr. Joseph Juran, a noted American quality authority, further developed Pareto's inadvertent discovery, and so named this phenomena the Pareto principle in Pareto's honor. Juran found that the Pareto principle applied to many different things such as absenteeism, defects, and accidents. He found that many things typically align themselves and follow the principle that 80% of problems are manifested in 20% of the items with the problem.

Suppose that a machine is experiencing faults, and we have been asked to look into the problem. We assemble the data and notice that the frequency of the faults is not the same every day. If we were to arrange the

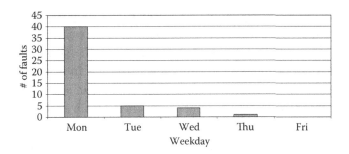

FIGURE 2.4
Number of faults by week.

data as a Pareto chart by day of the week, as in Figure 2.4, we see that the chart of this data validates what we believed was true. The Pareto chart gives a picture of the days of the week, and clearly shows us that we have a severe problem with faults on Monday, and then the faults gradually decrease as the week progresses, until Friday when they cease to exist. By knowing that Monday is the worst day for faults, we can focus our efforts on comparing what is unique or different on Monday compared to the best day of the week, Friday.

Likewise, if we are working on a problem with quality defects, for example, and we suspect operator differences, we can collect data on each operator and construct a Pareto chart to visually demonstrate the differences. Figure 2.5 is a Pareto chart displaying each operator's defect level. Clearly Jim has significantly more defects than the other three, and in particular Lisa. This suggests that there could be a work method difference between what Jim is doing compared to what Andy, Tom, and Lisa are doing. If we can study Jim's and Lisa's methods, find the differences or distinctions, and then modify Jim's method, then doesn't it make sense that Jim's defect level would be reduced to near the level of the other operators?

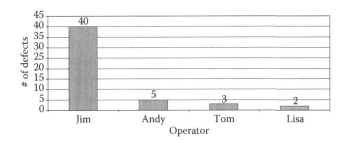

FIGURE 2.5
Number of defects by operator.

Pareto charts are really quite simple to create. Along the horizontal or x-axis, we simply place what we are comparing (e.g., operators, machines), and then place whatever we are measuring along the vertical or y-axis. Now what could be more straightforward than that? In Figure 2.5 we see that Jim has had forty defects, Andy five, Tom three, and Lisa two. The important thing to remember about Pareto charts, from a problem-solving perspective, is that if significant differences in the level of the response variable exists, then we must search for differences in methods (for operators) or functions (for machines) that created the difference in performance.

Although Pareto charts are easy to develop, most people don't use them effectively. In my first book, *Process Problem Solving: A Guide for Maintenance and Operations Teams*, I used an example of fiberglass panels that had a variety of defects on them [2]. We constructed a Pareto chart and found that blisters were the number one defect problem. From this Pareto, we spawned a second, lower level Pareto of part types and concluded that one of the six different part types examined (part J40) had 74% of the blisters. This allowed us to focus on this part type rather than working on all six parts. We then divided this part into six different physical zones and determined that Zone A contained 72% of the blisters. By using a series of Pareto charts, this team had a clear sense of direction and a focal point: it would focus its efforts on blisters on part J40 in Zone A. If the team was able to determine the root cause of these blisters on this part and in this zone, then it might be able to translate this to the other parts and other zones.

It's never easy to eat an elephant or an apple in one single bite, but if we take one bite at a time, we have a much better chance of succeeding. Multilevel Pareto charts help the team focus and prioritize its efforts.

2.3 CAUSE-AND-EFFECT DIAGRAM

Our third tool, the *cause-and-effect diagram*, or *fishbone diagram* (because its structure resembles the bones of a fish), is one of the most popular tools ever developed. It was created and developed by Dr. Kaoru Ishikawa, a noted Japanese consultant, and is also referred to as the Ishikawa diagram in his honor. A cause-and-effect diagram is a tool that helps identify, organize, and display possible causes of a specific problem. It graphically illustrates the relationship between a given outcome (the effect) and all

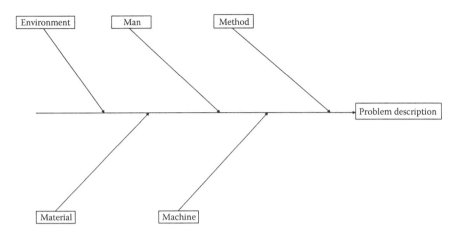

FIGURE 2.6
Cause-and-effect diagram.

the factors that might influence the outcome (the causes). The structure of the diagram helps the team think in a very systematic way, as it looks for potential causes of the problem it is trying to solve. Figure 2.6 is a typical layout of a cause-and-effect diagram.

The construction of a cause-and-effect diagram starts by identifying and defining the outcome or *effect* being studied (i.e., problem description), and placing it to the far right side of a straight line. We then establish main causal categories, such as man, method, machine, and materials, and place them at the end of diagonal lines drawn from the central spine of the fish, as is illustrated in Figure 2.6. For each of the main categories, we then identify other, more specific factors that could be the *causes of the effect*, and place them on offshoot bones from the diagonal lines. We continue to identify more detailed and more explicit causes, and then organize them on bones that come off the offshoot bones.

Figure 2.7 is a hypothetical cause-and-effect diagram for a person with diabetes whose blood sugar is out of control. Four major categories were selected (Food/Nutrition, Medicine, Exercise, and Person) and then more specific, potential causes for the out-of-control diabetes were added to each major category. These more specific secondary causes are seen as the smaller bones on the fish emanating from the major categories at the end of the diagonal lines as we attempt to zero in on our list of potential causes of the problem. Finally, even more specific causes are added. For example, under the category Exercise we see that the "level of exercise" is listed with "too low" and "none" completing this series of bones.

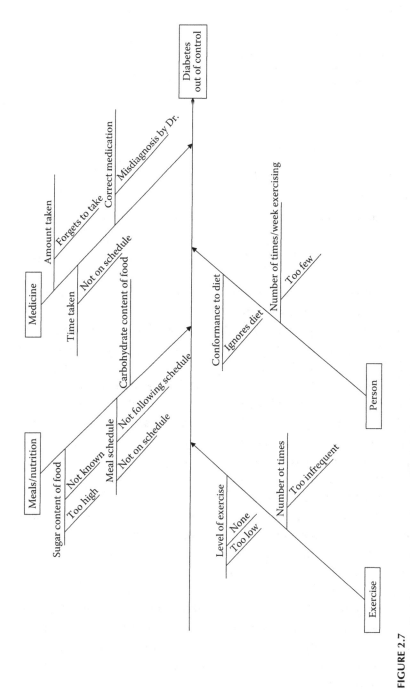

FIGURE 2.7

Cause-and-effect diagram for out-of-control diabetes.

The cause-and-effect diagram can be a very useful tool when attempting to identify potential causes of the problem at hand, if its development is done without bias and with an open mind. My advice to teams that are creating cause-and-effect diagrams is simple. No matter how ridiculous one of the potential causes put forth by a team member might be, do not question it! The fastest way to alienate a team member is to openly question their intelligence in front of the other team members. For this reason, without question, list all potential causes and not just the ones that happen to fall in line with your way of thinking. One very effective method I have used quite effectively as the team tries to identify potential root causes is to ask the team members the following question: If I were to ask you to make this problem appear, how would you do it? In other words, instead of trying to come up with potential causes, get the team members thinking about the things they could do to create the same problem they are attempting to solve. Try it, it works well.

2.4 CAUSAL CHAIN

The final tool we will be discussing in this chapter is the *causal chain*. When problems occur, we know that a chain of events has taken place to alter the performance of the process. We aren't always certain as to what happened, so we need some kind of tool or technique that will help us develop a theory as to what did happen. One of the most effective tools available for accomplishing this is the causal chain. Causal chains are stepwise evolutions of problem causes (Figure 2.8). Each step in the causal chain represents an object in either a normal or abnormal state. The object is placed

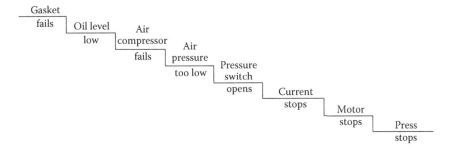

FIGURE 2.8
Single stairstep causal chain.

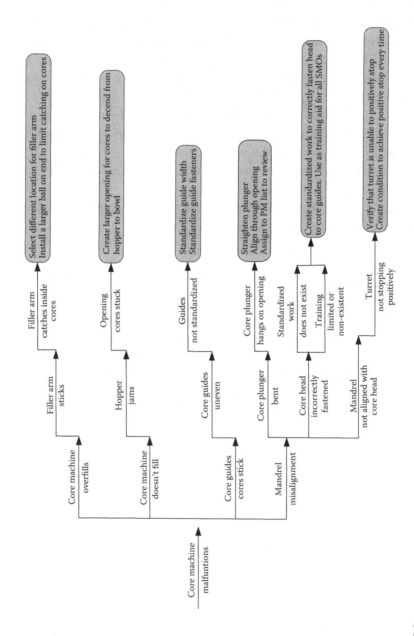

FIGURE 2.9
Multiple stairstep causal chain.

on the line to the far right of the chain, with the state it is in listed directly beneath it. So, in Figure 2.8, the object in distress is the press and its state is that it has stopped. Although we might use a cause-and-effect diagram to list the variety of reasons why the press stopped, it does not explain the causal mechanism that actually caused it.

In Figure 2.8 we see that a press has stopped and we ask the question why. The press stopped because the motor stopped. Why did the motor stop? Because the current has stopped flowing. We continue asking why until we reach the end of our chain, and find that the press stopped, because the motor stopped, because the current stopped, because the pressure switch opened, because the air pressure was too low, because the air compressor failed, because the oil level was too low, because of a gasket that failed. We have now developed a potential theory as to why the press stopped, and along the way we have identified objects or items (e.g., current, oil level) that we can test to prove or disprove our theory. Each step is the cause of the next step and the effect of the preceding step. That is, the information on the step to the left is always the cause of the information on the step to the right.

What if we have more than one potential cause? How do we handle that situation? The answer is simple. We just create additional, individual chains like the one in Figure 2.8 and place them along the y-axis as in Figure 2.9. This is an actual example from a team that was working on a core machine that was malfunctioning. Here the team brainstormed and came up with four different chains. Each individual chain is, in reality, a brief theory to prove or disprove, as to how the core machine was malfunctioning.

Ultimately, the team either eliminated the chain as a potential cause through testing or developed action items for each of the potential root causes. At the end of the day, the team performed all of the actions in the gray shaded boxes, and the problem was not only solved, but it was improved from its previous state.

Remember, the primary purpose of a causal chain is to develop a step-wise chain of events that explains why a particular performance shortfall exists. Once this is complete, hypotheses or theories can be formulated as to why a problem exists. Causal chains are, in my opinion, one of the simplest and effective, yet most underutilized tools available for a team to use.

3

A Structured Approach to Problem Solving

When a problem comes along, study it until you are completely knowledgeable. Then find that weak spot, break the problem apart, and the rest will be easy.

Norman Vincent Peale

All three of the problem types presented in Chapter 1—change-related, chronic, and hybrid—can be solved using the same basic structured and systematic problem-solving methodology. In the chapters that follow, we will look at a real problem that I was involved with and follow it to its successful conclusion using a systematic and structured approach, and then present the actual step-by-step approach one of my teams used to solve it. It is my belief that if you will follow the roadmap I have developed, then your level or frequency of solved problems will dramatically improve.

3.1 THE STRUCTURED APPROACH

This case study involves a company that manufactures flexible tanks used to hold volatile liquids. In the interior of the tank is a rubber product, referred to as an inner liner, that is coated with other materials that actually hold the liquids inside the tank, much like the inner liner of a tire holds air. The inner liner material has "always" had a problem with "splits" occurring on it in the early stages of the process and had resisted all efforts to date to find a root cause and eliminate it.

The split must be repaired before proceeding to the next step, because of the potential leak path it might create. To make matters worse, the split was not always detected during the inspection, prior to the tank being cured, creating a much more difficult postcure repair. It was a potentially serious problem, because of the aforementioned leak potential.

This particular problem had apparently been around for as long as anyone could remember, and everyone on the team had doubts that this problem could actually be solved. By asking one simple question during the first team meeting convinced me that it could in fact be solved. During the first meeting, I asked this question to the team that was assembled: "Have you ever produced a tank that did not have this problem?" The team members assured me that they routinely make tanks without this problem and that in fact only 40% of their tanks actually had splits in them. I confidently told them that if they can make one tank without the split, then we will solve the problem. From the looks of doubt that I received, it was apparent that they weren't buying what I was saying, so I had a room full of disbelievers.

In the next six chapters, we will take a look at how we did solve this problem by using the following *Problem Solving Roadmap*. The roadmap (Figure 3.1) is an amalgam of tools, techniques, and experience that I have used over the years to not only successfully solve problems but to also teach others. It has worked on a variety of problems, from a diversity of industries producing a multiplicity of products. The roadmap will work equally well for service companies and can also be used as a guide to process improvement. I think you will find that there is no equal to this roadmap when it comes to a detailed, step-by-step methodology for solving problems in a systematic way.

I cannot overstate the importance of following a logical, systematic, and structured approach to solving problems for a number of reasons. First, a systematic approach keeps the team focused and helps discourage a team from wandering aimlessly. Many times, I have witnessed teams struggling with a sense of direction or what to do next, but once they were presented with a roadmap to follow, they stayed on track and made significant and rapid progress. Second, using a structured approach helps the team understand what information is needed, and then facilitates the organization of data, thoughts, and information. It separates what's important from what isn't. Third, by using and following a systematic approach, with its logical progression of tasks and activities, the probability of finding the true root cause increases significantly. Finally, by using a structured approach in a

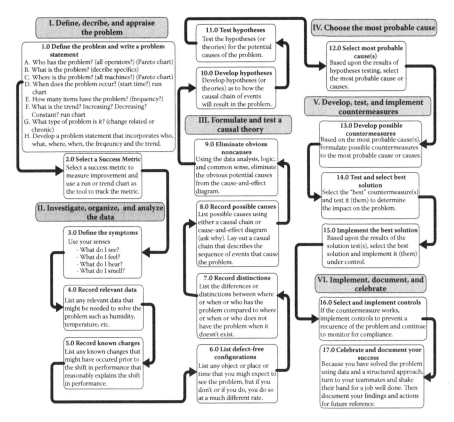

FIGURE 3.1
Problem Solving Roadmap.

team setting, the maximum utilization of resources will be achieved in the shortest period of time. In other words, problems get solved completely, in considerably much less time, with full participation of the team.

3.2 PROCESS IMPROVEMENT, SIX SIGMA, AND TOYOTA'S PRACTICAL PROBLEM SOLVING

Although the Problem Solving Roadmap was created to assist teams in solving problems, it is equally effective when used as a vehicle for *process improvement*. Not only is the roadmap in complete alignment with the Six Sigma methodology of define, measure, analyze, improve, and control, it is in alignment with the problem-solving teachings within Jeffrey Liker's

TABLE 3.1

Six Sigma and Toyota's Practical Problem Solving versus Problem Solving Roadmap

Six Sigma Element	Problem Solving Roadmap Step	Toyota's Practical Problem Solving
Define	I. Define, describe, and appraise the problem	1. Initial problem perception 2. Clarify the problem (the "real" problem) 3. Locate area/point of cause (where the problem physically occurs)
Measure	II. Collect data	
Analyze	III. Investigate, organize, and analyze the data IV. Formulate and test a causal theory V. Select the most probable cause	4. Investigation of the root cause by using 5 Whys
Improve	VI. Develop, test, and implement countermeasures	5. Develop countermeasures 6. Evaluate
Control	VII. Implement, document, and celebrate	7. Standardize

The Toyota Way [3]. All of the elements of the Problem Solving Roadmap coincide with the actions needed to improve processes. The implication here is that it isn't necessary to wait for a problem to be declared before using the roadmap. Table 3.1 summarizes these alignments.

Back to our problem solving, let's take a look at this process and see how this team solved the problem with split inner liners. As you go through this process, remember that this team had never received any substantial problem-solving training, but by diligently following the Problem Solving Roadmap, they were able to solve a problem that had plagued their company for years. The team was comprised of just ordinary people achieving extraordinary results by simply following the roadmap. I'm certain that you too can achieve extraordinary things.

4

Define, Describe, and Appraise the Problem

The most serious mistakes are not being made as a result of wrong answers. The truly dangerous thing is asking the wrong questions.

Peter Drucker

4.1 DEFINE, DESCRIBE, AND APPRAISE THE PROBLEM

Before we can begin to truly analyze and solve a problem, we really have to define, describe, and appraise the problem in simple terms everyone is familiar with and understands. This is an important first step because all of the work that follows will be focused on solving and correcting the problem as we have defined it. Peter Drucker's opening quote sums up what we have to do in this chapter: Ask the right questions.

Just what are these right questions? First, they are basic questions that will help the team develop a complete definition of the problem and allow the team to move forward. Without a complete problem definition, it will be virtually impossible to align a problem-solving team toward the ultimate solution to the problem. The answers to these questions form the basic framework for the team assigned to solve the problem. So, let's look at these problem questions.

What is the problem? That is, what specifically isn't working as we would like it to be, and what specifically is the defect or malfunction? If the problem is equipment related, we might ask, What is the machine that isn't working the way we want? and What, specifically, is the shortcoming in performance? Here we would name the machine or machines that aren't functioning correctly, and what the specific malfunction, fault or defect is.

In our case study, the first what (what specifically isn't working) was the inner liner material, and the second *what* (the defect or malfunction) was the split that was occurring in the liner material.

Where is the problem? With this question, we are attempting to define where the performance problem is geographically, and where on the object we are observing the problem. Again, if the problem is equipment related, we would define the facility location of the machine with the problem, as well as the exact location on the machine. Whenever possible, try to use a schematic of both the facility where the problem is and a drawing of the actual unit with the problem, so that you can mark the location directly on each of these.

In our case study, the first where (geographically) was at the cement post, and the second where (on the object) was on the inner liner material joint overlap for the most part (97% of the splits were occurring at the joint overlap).

When does the problem occur? Here we are looking for the timing of the problem from its inception, subsequent appearances of the problem, and specifically when in the operating cycle is the problem observed. When was the problem first observed (date and time)? When has it been observed since the onset of the problem (dates and times)? When, in the operating cycle of the unit, do we observe the problem (which process step)? For equipment problems, define the exact date and time that the problem was first observed, the exact dates and times it has malfunctioned since the onset of the problem, and at what stage of the normal process cycle is the problem observed. The most effective tool to utilize here is the trend or run chart, which has an axis (x-axis) for time and an axis (y-axis) for monitoring the level of the problem.

In our case study, the first when (first observation) was undefined, since the problem had reportedly been occurring for years. The second when (when since the first observation of the problem has the problem been observed) cannot totally be determined, since this has been an ongoing problem for a number of years, and no data was collected until this team began collecting it. The third when (when in the operating cycle) was after application of cement to the surface of the inner liner and after sitting overnight.

How many units or items have the problem? Since we are trying to define the magnitude of the problem, we need to know the extent to which the problem exists. That is, how many units are affected, and what percentage of any one unit is affected? For example, suppose you have five machines producing the same or similar products, and only one machine is affected by the performance problem. Here you make note that only machine A is impacted. The most effective tool to answer this question is the Pareto chart. The Pareto chart provides a graphical representation of the problem for everyone to see.

In our case study, approximately 20% to 30% of the tanks produced had the problem (Note: A run chart will be presented later to show the percentage of total tanks with the problem as a function of time), and the split could be the length of the joint or just a portion of it (the team saw both). This split was also observed at locations directly behind the joint, but this was seen on approximately only 3% of the tanks affected.

Who has the problem? If there are humans involved (i.e., operators), then we need to define exactly who the operators are with the problem. Suppose there are three operators, and only one is exhibiting the performance shortcoming. By defining this point, we can focus our attention on what the differences or distinctions are that will lead us to the root cause of the problem. Here we can use a Pareto chart or a simple matrix of operators.

In our case study, there are approximately ten inner liner operators and three cement operators who have produced tanks that had this defect. (Note: A Pareto chart will be presented later.)

Is the problem change-related, or is it a launch-related problem, or is it a hybrid of a change- and launch-related problem? This is important to determine, because our approach to solving the problem is uniquely different. In a change-related problem, we focus most of our efforts and attention on determining exactly what changed and when the change occurred. In a launch-related problem, the answer to the problem lies in accurately determining the differences or distinctions between where or when the problem occurs compared to when or where it doesn't. Or, in the event that the distinction is found to be a person, who has the problem compared to who doesn't have the problem.

In a change-related problem, our primary tool is a trend or run chart, while in a launch-related problem we utilize Pareto charts or matrices as a means of comparison. Of course, in a hybrid type problem, we use both the run chart and the Pareto chart.

In our case study, we were not certain as to whether this was a change-related problem, a launch-related problem, or a hybrid, because data had not been collected on inner liner splits in the past. Because of this uncertainty, the problem was treated as though it was a hybrid problem and could therefore, be the result of changes, distinctions, or both.

What is the *trend* of the problem? That is, is the problem increasing, decreasing, or remaining constant? The trend or run chart developed earlier will answer this question.

In our case study, the trend, at least for the period of time data had been collected, was relatively constant or at least continuous. The run chart will be presented later since the team had not yet begun to chart the information when I arrived.

Develop a *problem* statement. The final step in the definition of the problem is to develop a problem statement that incorporates all of the information we have just developed (i.e., the what, the where, the when, the who, the magnitude/frequency, and the trend) into a single statement that fully describes the problem we are trying to solve.

In our case study, before I had arrived, the team had simply stated "splits in the inner liner material" as the problem. If the team had followed the flowchart, then the problem statement might have been, "A split is occurring on the inner liner material, on approximately 20% to 30% of the tanks, after application of inner liner cement, and after sitting for 24 hours. All operators have had tanks with splits, and the trend is constant." Remember the problem statement provides the direction for the entire team, and if it is complete enough, the team will have a much better idea of how to proceed. The difference between the team's original statement of the problem and the one I have presented here is that mine is based upon answers to the questions presented in this first step of the problem solving roadmap.

4.2 SELECT A SUCCESS METRIC

One of the most frequently missed steps in a problem-solving event is the failure of the team to develop a quantitative way of knowing if what they have done has impacted the results. I often hear people saying things like "it looks better" or "it seems to be better." For goodness sakes, don't guess and don't give us your opinion; measure your progress. For this reason, I have added a new step to my approach to problem solving and that is the development of what I call a *success metric*.

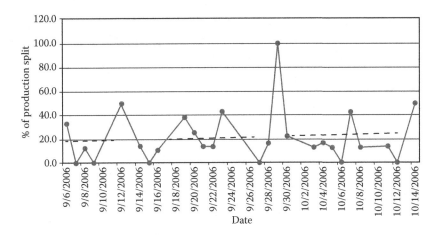

FIGURE 4.1
Run chart of percent of production with split liners.

The success metric can be as simple as the number of objects with the problem as a function of time, or it can be the percent of production with the problem, or any other metric that the team agrees will let them know if improvement has been achieved. In any event, you want to be able to relate the response of any changes you might make to the level of the problem. The trend chart or run chart is the best tool to accomplish this. You will recall from the last chapter that the trend chart displays time (hours, days, weeks, etc.) along the x-axis and the level of what you are measuring along the y-axis. These charts are simple to create, and they permit the team to record the actual changes made directly on the chart, making it completely visible to everyone.

In our case study, I prepared a run chart (using Excel) that was used by the team to track its progress (Figure 4.1). As you can see, the x-axis represents time and the y-axis is the percent of production with inner liner splits. Since the team had no historical data to understand when the problem had begun, we first had to establish a data collection system to capture data on the defect, which we did. Once the success metric was established, it was time to move to step 3, the definition of symptoms.

5

Investigate, Organize, and Analyze the Data

One who returns to a place, sees it with new eyes. Although the place may not have changed, the viewer inevitably has. For the first time, things invisible before, become suddenly visible.

Louis L'Amour (*Bendigo Shafter*)

5.1 RECORD THE SYMPTOMS

Solving problems is very similar to a forensics expert trying to solve a crime. One of the first steps taken by crime scene investigators is to seal off the crime scene and begin collecting evidence that might be used to solve the crime later. The investigators might dust the scene for fingerprints, or take pictures, or even record blood spatter patterns. The reason they do this is to attempt to reconstruct the crime through the available evidence. They may or may not use all of this evidence in court, but it is available to help explain what might have happened.

When we attempt to solve a problem, we are, in effect, crime scene investigators. We look at the symptoms of the problem, and then try to logically tie what we find to some reasonable explanation of the causal chain of events. We use our senses of sight, touch, hearing, and smell (and sometimes taste), then record what our senses tell us. Our next step is to ask some basic questions relative to our senses:

- What do I see when the problem is present or just prior to the onset of the problem?
- What do I feel when the problem is present or just prior to the onset of the problem?
- What do I hear when the problem is present or just prior to the onset of the problem?
- What do I smell when the problem is present or just prior to the onset of the problem?
- What do I taste (sometimes) when the problem is present or just prior to the onset of the problem?

Recording what our senses are conveying to us can give us valuable information as we move through our problem-solving process. Suppose we have a condition where compressed air is no longer being supplied to a production machine. A team is assigned to this problem, and after constructing the problem statement and the success metric, it begins the search for symptoms. One of the first things the team might do is to look in the compressor room to see if the compressor has stopped running. When the team members arrive at the compressor, maybe they find oil on the floor around the compressor. The oil is a symptom of the problem.

The team continues to search the area around the compressor and maybe find, through touching the compressor, that the temperature appears to be hotter than it should be, another symptom. Maybe the team smells a peculiar odor normally associated with an overheating condition, a third symptom. Whatever the team members find, it is important to record these valuable "clues," as they attempt to reconstruct the sequence of events that led to the stoppage of compressed air.

In our case study, the team went to the production floor and made observations relative to the defect as follows:

1. There appears to be an excess amount of cement on the inner liner material, but especially in the joint area. This was especially true based upon the number of "runs" of cement and other solutions observed. The tank looked just like a wall that had too much paint on it.
2. When the defect appears, it is on or near the joint, and usually in the curved portion of the plaster form.

3. The surface of the inner liner appeared tackier to the touch on tanks with the defect.
4. The team did not hear or smell anything abnormal and we certainly didn't taste anything.

5.2 RECORD RELEVANT DATA

If you've ever been involved in a problem-solving activity, you have probably run into a situation where a question came up that you couldn't answer because no information was available. For example, suppose one of your teammates is convinced that humidity or viscosity are factors that could contribute to a particular defect, only to discover that you have no humidity or viscosity data. It can be pretty frustrating, can't it? My recommendation is that you collect as much information as is available, as close to the onset of the problem as possible. In the end, it may not be needed, but if it isn't collected and it is needed later, there isn't much you can do about it. The guidelines for collecting this data are simple. If there is even a remote possibility that it could contribute to the problem, then collect it. Having said this, let me give a word of caution. Don't ever let the desire to collect data interfere with the problem-solving process. Too often I have seen an inordinate amount of effort placed on data collection and too little placed on solving the problem.

In our case study, we recorded the names (initials) of the inner liner and cement operators, the lot number and date of the rubber inner liner material, and the temperature and humidity in the shop. As it turned out, humidity was an important factor for the team, but any or all of these factors may or may not have been used later, but at least we had them if they were needed.

5.3 RECORD KNOWN CHANGES

As discussed earlier, one type of problem emerges after a change has been made somewhere in the process. We use a trend or run chart to determine approximately when this change in performance occurred, and then look for documented process changes that happened prior to when the problem started. I say approximately, because I have witnessed too many examples of changes that occurred months prior to the onset of the problem, and there may or may not be complete documentation available.

One example of this might be a problem that is tied to humidity or temperature. Suppose, for example, that a process change was made in July or August in Alabama, and the problem is caused by low temperatures. Its effects might not be observed until December, January, or February, since those are the only months that get cold in Alabama. My advice is that any change made to the process, within at least the last six months, should be recorded and tracked. Six months is simply a guideline, based on my experiences, but it certainly isn't a hard and fast rule. I have even seen an example of a change made almost a year prior to the appearance of the problem found to be the root cause of the problem. When in doubt, record the change.

Where should the problem-solving team record the changes? My advice is very simple. Record all changes directly onto the run chart. The reason I recommend this is simple. By recording all known changes on the same document as the defect rate (i.e., the run chart), it is much easier to directly visualize the impact of the change if it is tied to increases or decreases in the level of the problem. In Chapter 3, in the case of the engineering backlog, we saw the full impact of recording the change directly onto the run chart.

In our case study, there were no known, or at least no documented, changes that had been made prior to the onset of the problem, whenever the onset was years ago.

5.4 SEARCH FOR AND LIST DEFECT-FREE CONFIGURATIONS

Suppose you have three operators that produce the same product, and only one of the three is producing a particular defect. Wouldn't you be interested in knowing why one is while the other two aren't? Or suppose you have two machines producing identical products, and only one of the machines is producing a defect, or if it isn't, the defect rate is significantly lower than the other one. Couldn't knowledge of why there is a difference help you understand the cause of the problem? Well the answer is a resounding yes!

The machines or people who are performing closer to or at the expected level of performance are called *defect-free configurations* (DFCs). They are the answer to the question, Where or when would you expect to see the problem, but you aren't? If DFCs exist, they can be very valuable to the team, because they can shorten and decomplicate the actions of the team. DFCs can be people, machines, materials, processes, systems, and so forth, and the fact that they exist is proof positive that a problem can be either completely solved or its effects can be minimized.

In our case study, the team had already developed a cause-and-effect diagram by the time I had arrived and had begun the process of eliminating potential causes. As I sat in my first meeting with this team, I noticed that one of the causes the team had identified were the operators that produce the first part of the tank. It seemed strange to me that the team had already eliminated them as a potential cause. I sat silently, but wondered to myself how or by what criteria they had concluded that operators were not the cause of the effect they were observing (i.e., splits in the inner liner material).

After the meeting, I stopped the team leader and asked him how they had concluded that operators (or their methods) could not have caused the problem. He simply told me that based upon their experience, operators were not an issue. Apparently, this decision had been hotly debated, but in the end, he himself decided to remove it as a cause.

I decided to follow up on this point and look at any data that might be available that might either confirm that the operators were not a factor in this defect or confirm that there was an operator correlation to the defect. I started with the first step in the process where the inner liner is applied to a plaster form. I found that there were ten to twelve operators producing tanks at various work stations.

I created the Pareto Chart shown in Figure 5.1, and as you can see, there was not one operator that stood out as a DFC, so maybe the leader was right after all about operators not being a cause of the problem.

I then went to the next step in the process where operators apply a cement to the surface of the inner liner material to prepare it for later steps in the process. Again, I created a Pareto chart to determine if there was a cement operator relationship to the problem of split inner liners (see Figure 5.2). Much to my surprise, one operator had significantly more split inner liners than the other two.

But what if the operator with the most defects also produces the most tanks? Could that be the reason he has more split inner liners? Again, I went to the data and prepared a Pareto chart (Figure 5.3). Yes, he had made more tanks, but his rate of failure was the key point here. The percentage

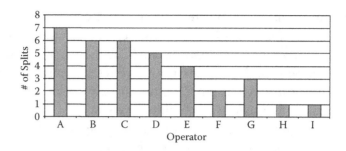

FIGURE 5.1
Pareto chart for number of inner liner splits by inner liner operator.

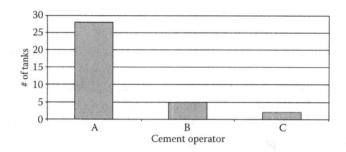

FIGURE 5.2
Pareto chart for number of tanks with split inner liners by cement operator.

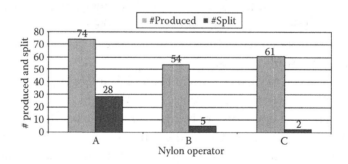

FIGURE 5.3
Total produced and number of total inner liner splits by cement operator.

of his production with split inner liners was significantly higher than the other two operators. That is, operator A had almost 80% of the defects but had produced only 39% of the tanks. Operator C had only 6% of the defects and had produced 32% of the tanks. Because of this finding, I could not rule out operators as a potential cause of the problem and decided to meet with the team to review my findings. In my opinion, operator C should be considered a defect-free configuration and the team agreed.

I continued my look for DFCs and surprisingly I found tank types that did not exhibit this same problem, which was contrary to what I had been told. Figure 5.4 is a Pareto chart of tank types with and without inner liner splits, and it was clear that although there were two tank types that stood out from the rest, as far as having the defect, there were a number of other tank types that did not have any split inner liners during the three weeks since data had been collected.

Even though this problem of split inner liners had been around for years without resolution, I felt very confident that based upon the emergence of these two examples of DFCs, this problem could be resolved. If these tanks could be produced without having splits, then all of them could be.

At the next team meeting, I presented the information and explained the concept of a defect-free configuration, and all of the team members agreed to keep operators on the cause-and-effect diagram as a possible cause of split inner liners. The team had learned a valuable lesson regarding the importance of making decision based upon data, rather than feelings and experience.

The importance of searching for, and hopefully finding, DFCs cannot be overstated here. DFCs offer hope to the team for resolution of a problem. If a team can determine why the DFCs exist, then they clearly can impact, at least, the level of the problem if not completely eliminate it. DFCs tell us that there is something uniquely different about where or when you see the problem compared to where or when you don't. If you can pinpoint these differences, then you are on the road to problem resolution.

Before we leave defect-free configurations, however, there is one last point I want to make. I mentioned that DFCs tell us that there is something

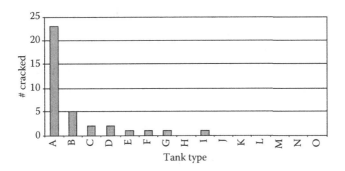

FIGURE 5.4
Pareto chart of number of tanks with inner liner splits by tank type.

uniquely different about where or when we see the problem. Suppose that you create a run chart and you notice that the defect is only observed on Mondays and Tuesdays or between 8:00 am and 5:00 pm, what would that tell us? Defect-free configurations can also be related to the time we observe the problem. Suppose, for example, that we researched a problem and discovered that a particular problem only occurred on the first shift of a three-shift operation; wouldn't that be important to know? Of course, it would be! It implies that there is something different going on in the process during the first shift, doesn't it? It could be a temperature difference, an operator difference, or something else we hadn't considered. So please, when you are looking for a DFC, consider the subject of time. Now let's move on to the next step in the process: our search for distinctions.

5.5 STUDY AND RECORD DISTINCTIONS

You will recall from our earlier discussion on launch-related problems that solutions to these types of problems are many times found in the distinctions between where or when you have the problem compared to where or when you don't have the problem. Distinctions are found in a variety of ways, including direct observations of operators (including videotaping) if the team suspects differences in operator work methods or machine functions; comparing drawings or schematics if there are equipment differences are suspected; differences in materials if materials are suspected; or any other head to head comparisons that might demonstrate differences between the operators, machines, materials, and so on. Remember, we are looking for things we observe when or where we have the problem compared to when or where we don't have the problem, in that order.

In our case study, you will remember that we had identified two examples of defect-free configurations, tank types, and cement operators. The team observed the two tanks that exhibited the problem most frequently, compared them to tanks that never have the problem, and discovered an important difference: the position of the overlapped inner liner joint, or seam, where the two ends of the inner liner material meet. On the two tank types with the problem, the seam always terminates directly above the break area (i.e., corners) of the plaster form. On the tanks without the problem, the joint seemed to always terminate in flat areas of the form. Was this an important distinction? The team was sure it was, but in this step, we are only looking for differences and not why the distinction may or may not be important. The team recorded this finding as a distinction.

In the case of the three cement operators, the team elected to videotape the operators' motions, techniques, and methods, and then review the videotapes as a team to look for differences. This was done and the team reviewed the videos and compared the operator who was having 80% of the split inner liners to the operator that only had 6%. The team discovered major differences in work methods, especially as it related to the amount of cement applied to the inner liner. The operator who had 80% of the defects applied significantly more cement than the operator who had only 6% of the defects. In addition, the team observed differences in the method of application of the cement and recorded each difference for future use. Again, we are only looking for differences and not the reason why the difference might be important. This is an extremely important thing to remember, because differences should only be discounted or accepted after discussions later in the process.

5.6 BRAINSTORM AND RECORD POSSIBLE CAUSES

Somewhere in the maze of symptoms, changes, defect-free configurations, and distinctions lies the reason or explanation of why the problem exists. Solving a problem is very much like putting together a jigsaw puzzle with pieces of information that fit together to form a logical cause. The key to generating potential causes is to ask the question why. Why would this distinction or change have produced the problem? Although there are several excellent tools available to the team to develop potential causes, my favorite is the cause-and-effect diagram or, as it is commonly known, the fishbone diagram, because its structure resembles the skeleton of a fish. Typically, major categories such as man, method, material, and machine that represent possible cause areas are connected to the central spine of the fish, and then smaller bones that represent more specific causes are added. The cause-and-effect diagram is a good visual representation of cause-and-effect relationships that aid in the development of potential causes that produce the observed effect.

Figure 5.5 is an example of a cause-and-effect diagram that was developed for our problem of split inner liners on tanks. The team created five major categories (i.e., Environment, Operator, Work Method, Material,

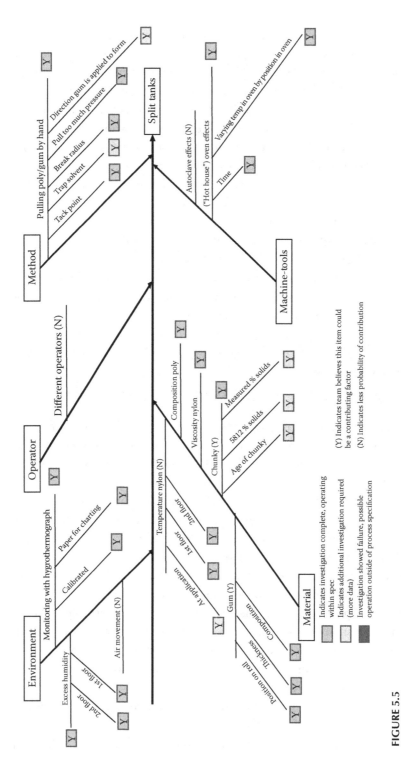

FIGURE 5.5

Cause-and-effect diagram for split tanks.

and Machine-Tools), and then brainstormed a comprehensive list of potential causes. Remember, not all of these potential causes will be responsible for the problem occurring, but somewhere within this list is the cause.

It is important not to reject any idea that a team member presents, even though it may seem irrelevant, simply because a rejection during a brainstorming session can have a negative effect on the team's creative juices and harmony. No matter how far-fetched the idea a teammate may present, list it on the cause-and-effect diagram. There will be plenty of time in the next step to remove it.

Cause-and-effect diagrams can be custom designed to fit any kind of problem, and there are numerous books available that go into detail on various techniques that can be used to supplement this tool. Our team also developed a color-coded visual technique that helped track progress on testing of possible causes later in the process. A colored box was added at the end of each fishbone, with different colors meaning different things. Green meant that the investigation into the potential cause was complete because it was found to be operating within specification. A yellow box meant that additional investigation is required or more data is needed. Red meant that the investigation showed failure or a possible operation outside the process specification. The team also used a "Y" or "N" to indicate whether it believed that the item was a potential contributing factor or not. As you can see, most of the boxes are labeled as a Y and most are green.

5.7 ELIMINATE OBVIOUS NONCAUSES

As mentioned earlier, not all of the possible causes listed on the cause-and-effect diagram will survive the logic, experience, and data in this step. Eliminating possible causes from the cause-and-effect diagram, must only come through analyzing data, uncovering facts, having discussions, and achieving a consensus among team members. Notice I didn't say that to eliminate a possible cause everyone on the team must agree. We would certainly like that to be the case, but in reality it doesn't always happen. What must be done when one or more members don't agree with the majority of the team is to agree to rethink the point later if the team fails to solve the problem. We certainly don't ever want to alienate any team member,

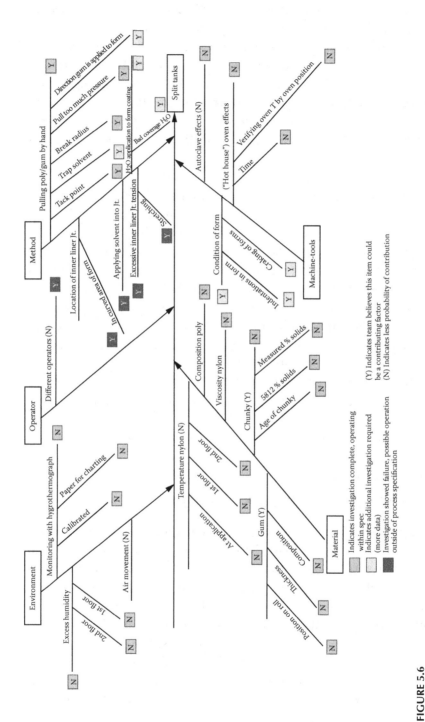

FIGURE 5.6

Cause-and-effect diagram for split tanks after assessment.

so my suggestion is to seek an amicable agreement and then move on with the process.

The team began the process of eliminating potential causes by starting with Environment in Figure 5.5. Since we have already shown that split liners were happening primarily with one cement operator, logically can't we conclude that humidity didn't spontaneously surround operator A and effect only him? So, we can eliminate humidity from our consideration of root causes, unless there are reasons to believe otherwise. Likewise, since all of the operators were using the same materials and tools, logically, can't both of those categories be eliminated as well? So, what we are left with is two primary categories, Operator and Method.

Our inner liner team went through this process and then updated its cause-and-effect diagram, as in Figure 5.6. In this team's cause-and-effect diagram, if the factor is not considered a possible cause, then a small green box with an N (indicating not a possible cause) is placed beside the possible cause. As you can see, the only categories that are still regarded as possible causes are Operator, Method, and part of Machine-Tools. When this step is complete, we then move on to the next step: developing hypotheses.

6

Formulate and Test a Causal Theory

It is a capital mistake to theorize before one has data. Insensibly one begins to twist facts to suit theories, instead of theories to suit facts.

Arthur Conan Doyle

6.1 DEVELOP A HYPOTHESIS

To develop a hypothesis is to develop a theory as to the sequence of events that led to the reason or reasons why a problem appeared. Of the tools available to the team, the causal chain is, for me, the most effective. It is one thing to create a long list of potential causes, like you would with a cause-and-effect diagram, but it is quite another to create the actual chain of events that produced the effect.

Causal chains are stepwise evolutions of problem causes. Again, the thought process behind theory development starts with the problem at hand and then, working backward, asking the question why until we arrive at a potential root cause. Each step represents an object in a normal or abnormal state, and is the cause of the next step and the effect of the preceding step. That is, the information on the step to the left is always the cause of the information on the step to the right. In creating the causal chain, we are attempting to not only find the cause or causes of the effect we have observed, but also the series, or string of events, that happened to create the problem.

When creating causal chains, or developing hypotheses, we always start our journey with the symptoms of the problem, but we also have to consider the impact of changes, defect-free configurations (DFCs), and distinctions. Our theory or theories must satisfy or explain what we have listed in each of these categories of information.

In the case of the split inner liner, we had determined that there were two DFCs: the type of tank and the operators who applied the cement to the inner liner. We then studied both of these DFCs and determined the distinctions or differences by comparing where we had the problem to where we did not have the problem. We must now use all of this information available to us, to formulate our hypotheses as to why these things (symptoms, changes, DFCs, and distinctions) could explain the problem. We combine our possible causes from our cause-and-effect diagram with all of our other information, and then develop a coherent theory or hypothesis as to the root cause or causes. Keep in mind you will usually have more than one theory of causation.

The number of theories a team develops is completely dependent upon the number of legs that exist on the causal chain, which is, in turn, dependent upon the array of symptoms, changes, defect-free configurations, and distinctions the team comes up with. Like I said, solving problems is much like putting the pieces of a jigsaw puzzle together to form a complete picture of the problem. So now that we have our pieces of our puzzle and have arranged them into a theory of sorts, we now turn our attention to proving or disproving what we have assembled.

Figure 6.1 is the causal chain that was developed by the problem-solving team working on the splitting inner liner. The team started with an abbreviated problem statement, and proceeded from right to left in a stepwise fashion, asking why a particular effect would occur.

The causal chains were then used to develop two theories as to why the inner liner was splitting. One of the theories that the team developed (taken from the bottom-most chain) is, "The inner liner is splitting, because it deteriorates when excessive organic solvent in the cement is applied to it by the operator." The other theory was, "Tension in the inner liner becomes excessive as it is stretched around the breaks in the form." In this step, we are only interested in creating the theories, not testing them, so we are finished with this step.

6.2 TEST YOUR HYPOTHESES

Just as if you were a mad scientist in a laboratory working on a new theory, so too must you prove what you have imagined to be true. You have given

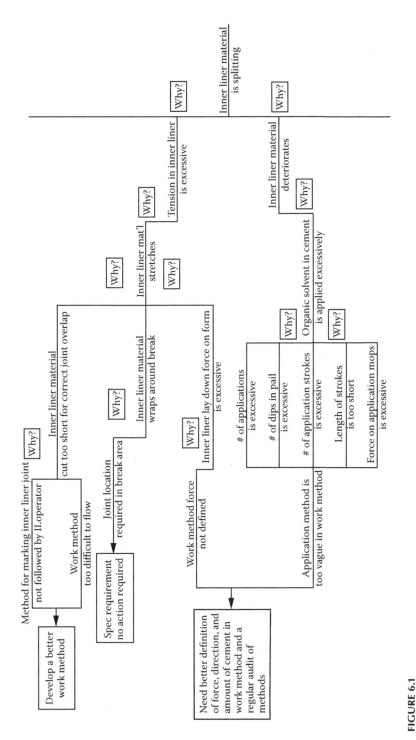

FIGURE 6.1
Inner liner splitting causal chain.

much thought to your theory, which was based on concrete data, observations, and intuition, and you are now ready to put your theory to the test. You know that proving your theory must withstand all attempts to disprove it, so you take your time thinking about how best to test it. Testing involves fully understanding the causal mechanism that led you to your theory, and then either setting up a series of tests or making the defect occur under controlled conditions.

In the case of the inner liners that split, the team had developed two primary theories that had to be tested. The first theory involved the joint being placed under tension as it was stretched around the corners of the plaster form. The team concluded there were two choices on the tests it could run. Either the joint could be moved into an area of less tension (i.e., a flat area on the form), or a tank type that already had the joint in a flat area could have the joint moved into the curved area of the form. The team elected to use the former rather than the latter simply because it wanted to improve a bad condition rather than worsen a good condition. I agreed with them.

The second theory revolved around the volume of cement applied to the inner liner material. Again, the team had two choices, and again it elected to attempt to improve a bad condition by instructing the operator with the highest proportion of splits to apply the same amount of cement as the best operator. Again, I agreed with the team, because to my way of thinking it is always a better choice when you are moving toward improvement. Having said that, there is an equal and opposite argument that would tell you it is always better to create the defect rather than do things to improve it during the testing phase. In some cases, I agree with this viewpoint, but in this case I did not.

The team chose to test the first theory, the one that involves tension on the inner liner joint as it passes around the curved area of the plaster form. The team could have selected the tank type with the highest proportion of split inner liners to study, but because the production requirements were low on this tank, the team instead elected to study the tank type that had both the highest number of defects and the highest production requirements. The rationale was that the higher build rate would provide the opportunity for faster results, and I agreed.

The team received approval to move the joint from the engineering group, then moved the joint away from the curved area of the form into a flat area. The results came almost immediately, in that three of the tanks displayed splits within the first day. But now, instead of the splits being at the joint as before, they were now located in the liner material directly above the curved part of the form but not at the joint. This sort of confirmed the tension theory, but the team was not satisfied. The team observed the first step in the build process again, where the inner liner is placed on the form. The team noted that the first-stage operators fold the liner material back onto itself, so that they are able to refresh the form to provide a tacky surface upon which to stick the inner liner to the form. The team concluded that this folding action probably caused a permanent deformation in the liner material and weakened it, and since this is now the area under tension, it is now susceptible to splitting. The team was actually happy to see the splits in the liner material, because it now had a much better understanding of the factors that create the splitting.

The team now turned its attention to the theory that excess cement (actually, the organic solvent in the cement) was attacking and deteriorating the liner material. The team wanted to make this a learning experience for the operators involved, so all three cement operators were invited to view the video of themselves. The team explained to the operators that they were looking for differences in work methods and specifically the volume of cement being applied. The operators watched intently, and shortly into the video, the operator who had the highest rate of liner splitting said that he noticed that he was applying much more of the cement than the other operators. The other two operators agreed and one of them asked which method was better. The team showed the operators the data for the first time on splitting, and all three operators immediately understood how much cement needed to be applied and how to apply it. The results were immediate, as the number of split inner liners was significantly reduced to near zero.

7
Choose the Most Probable Cause

When solving problems, dig at the roots, instead of just hacking at the leaves.

Anthony J. D'Angelo

7.1 POTENTIAL PROBLEM-SOLVING TRAPS

Solving problems isn't always as straightforward as some tools and techniques might lead you to believe, because in reality there are unforeseen obstacles that can tend to cloud the issue. There are problem-solving *traps*, or pitfalls, that lie in wait that will deceive and mislead the problem-solving team. Although you can't really eliminate these traps, you must be mindful that they exist. Like a well-polished con man, these traps will deceive you if you aren't careful, so be aware of their existence. These traps include:

1. Erroneous information, facts, or data
2. Defective measurement tools or gauges
3. Defective input material,
4. Defective replacement parts
5. Incorrect drawings or schematics
6. Incorrect logic on your part
7. Forcing the pieces to fit the puzzle
8. Desire to believe

Let's look at each one in more detail to better understand them.

Erroneous information. In my years of working on problems, using faulty or incorrect information is perhaps the most common pitfall or trap that occurs. It's usually unintentional, but sometimes faulty information is deliberately given to the team for whatever reason. Sometimes this is done to deliberately sabotage a problem-solving effort to make someone look bad, and other times it is done for personal gain, such as an operator wanting time off. Most of the time, however, erroneous information is received and accepted because we don't check it out before we use it. I always make it a practice to collect additional data to verify the data.

Defective measurement tools or gauges. Things aren't always as they seem. Believe it or not, everything that you believe to be true actually isn't sometimes, especially when the measurement tool you are using is giving you erroneous results. It does happen all too frequently, particularly when you don't have a good gauge control program in place. My advice to you is that if you don't have a gauge control program, then you should be wary of and suspicious of the results.

I was helping a team that was working on a closed mold fiberglass press that had a "hot oil" problem. The team had done an analysis and implemented a solution, but the problem persisted. The team was at an impasse, until I suggested checking the process gauges, just in case one might be dysfunctional. The team did and found that one of the pressure gauges was giving falsely low-pressure readings. The gauge was replaced and the pressure was adjusted into the proper operating range, fixing the problem. Keep in mind that when I say gauges, I mean handheld and/or gauges mounted on equipment.

Defective input material. Materials that have been understood and tagged to be good that are, in fact, bad or out of spec can lead a team on a wild goose chase. Incorrect raw or in-process material characteristics that affect the final product characteristics can lead your team to the wrong conclusions. I remember a team working on a problem with the flow of sheet molding compound (SMC) in a closed molded press. One of the key input characteristics that relates to flow is the viscosity of the input product. Seeing that the product had been accepted by the quality assurance (QA) lab, the team assumed that the product had acceptable viscosity. The material was rechecked and it was found that the viscometer being used to check the product was malfunctioning, thus giving the false assumption of good input material. Once the team knew this, it selected a different batch of product with "known" acceptable viscosity, and the problem was solved.

Defective replacement parts. Although this trap is similar to defective input material, this trap comes sealed in a new box, so how could it be wrong? It's another faulty assumption because we know from past experience that just because the packaging is sealed doesn't guarantee anything. I have seen this trap happen time and time again, so my advice is use logic. If you logically suspect that the cause of a problem is a defective part, but when you replace it, the problem remains, then test the part for functionality. The most common example is a burned out light bulb.

Incorrect drawings or schematics. Inaccurate equipment drawings or schematics are a much bigger problem than you might think. Many times, modifications are made to machines or equipment and the drawings are either not revised or are revised and not distributed. When the changes involve electrical circuits, this can be a very dangerous condition. It is imperative that all changes and updates to equipment, or even updates to work methods, are communicated first, and then filed (manually or electronically). In addition, a purge of the old documentation must be completed.

Incorrect logic. Even though your team has thought through the problem carefully, it is possible that the reasoning used by the team, or even one or more of the assumptions made, could simply be incorrect. It is always a good idea to have someone who is not involved in the problem-solving activity review the work of the team, just to see if he or she arrives at the same conclusions. It's not a sign of weakness, but rather a sign of strength.

Forcing the pieces to fit the puzzle. Although this trap seems difficult to believe, a team can actually force fit information to a problem profile that fits a problem cause without ever realizing it is happening. This usually happens when one person has a preconceived notion of what caused the problem. In order to guard against this trap, always check your logic to make certain that no puzzle pieces are missing.

Desire to believe. Sometimes facts and data are ignored or discounted solely because of one's desire to believe what they believe. Individual personalities, such as an inflated sense of self-worth, are usually the reasons this trap is seen. The belief and assertions that someone couldn't possibly be wrong is sometimes difficult to rise above, because it usually comes with such strong emotion. The remedy or cure for this behavior is to simply base your conclusions on documented facts.

Do not take any of these traps flippantly, because they are real and if their existence is ignored, a problem-solving exercise can be derailed. As you are trying to select the most probable cause, please consider these traps.

7.2 SELECT THE MOST PROBABLE CAUSE

If the testing for root cause was credible, well-conceived, and executed as planned, and your logic and conclusions were thought through well, then the results of the testing should clarify and illuminate the most probable, or most likely, cause of the problem. It is important to remember that sometimes problems have more than one cause, but typically a single root cause results in the problem.

Suppose, however, that after testing you still have more than one potential root cause, what then? Here is where relationships and logic enters into the picture. Suppose that you have three operators performing the same function, and two of them are either not experiencing the problem or are, but at a significantly lower frequency. Logic would tell you that something in the work method of the operator with the problem is causing the problem. In making this assumption, you have virtually eliminated systemic factors that equally affect all of the operators.

By the same token, if the problem is only observed on one of three machines, and each operator routinely runs each of the three machines, then you would conclude that something in the makeup or setup of the machine with the problem is different than the other two machines. Again, logic tells you that systemic factors are not the cause of the problem. Things like temperature and humidity could be discounted, unless you have reason to believe that the machine with the problem is subjected to operating conditions that the other two aren't.

It is absolutely imperative that the team uses logical reasoning when eliminating potential causes. Never eliminate a cause unless you understand completely why you are. For example, you will recall from the causal chain exercise that the team identified tension on the inner liner as one potential cause and excess cement (actually, it was the organic solvent in the cement) as the other. The question the team had to answer was, "If the amount of cement being applied to the liner material was not excessive, would splits still occur as a result of tension?"

If we go back to our Pareto chart of cement operators, then we have a partial answer to that question. Remember, one operator had almost 80% of the total inner liner splits, so the underlying cause appears to be excessive cement. But what about the other 20% of the failures? Since the other operators also had splits, albeit at a much lower frequency, we might conclude that either tension on the inner liner joint or excessive cement material applied to the surface of the liner material caused the splitting. But what if the other two operators in question sometimes apply excessive cement? Could that have caused the other 20% of the splits? The answer to this question will only come by auditing all of the operator work methods to make certain that all operators use the proper techniques and then apply the proper amount of cement.

In this case, the team discovered that the other two other operators did, in fact, occasionally apply more than the recommended amount of cement, especially when they were in a rush to complete the tank. When the team discussed this observation with all three of the operators, the operators responded accordingly by using care when applying the cement, and the level of split inner liners went to zero and the problem was solved. The final conclusion of the team was that the single root cause was excessive application of cement to the inner liner.

The team felt good that it had successfully solved this problem and there was a feeling of euphoria at the next team meeting. But just like the Grinch who stole Christmas, I told the team members that they were not yet finished, because I didn't agree with their conclusion. I knew that excess cement was the apparent cause, but they still had to answer the question of why the operators were applying too much of the cement. The team sat motionless, looking at each other and me, in disbelief until I asked one final question, "Why did the operators apply too much cement?" Their disbelief immediately turned to understanding. The team realized immediately that if the work method had specified the correct amount of cement, and if there had been regular audits to ensure that the correct work method was actually being accomplished, then the problem probably would never have occurred. The team agreed and began discussing the solution to this problem, which leads us to the next step in our problem-solving process.

8

Develop, Test, and Implement Solutions

It's so much easier to suggest solutions, when you don't know too much about the problem.

Malcolm Forbes

8.1 DEVELOP POSSIBLE SOLUTIONS

We have gone through the first four major sections of the roadmap, and have just identified and chosen the most probable cause, so it is now time to talk about what kind of solution best fits this problem. In developing a solution, we want one that is robust over a wide range of operating conditions. In short, we want to make a change to the way we are currently doing things that will, first, stop the performance issue and, second, preclude or prevent the problem from returning.

8.2 FACTORS TO CONSIDER

There are several important factors that must be considered when deciding upon the right solution to implement. The old expression "there's more than one way to skin a cat" is really true when it concerns developing solutions to problems. For example, we want a solution that will be easy and practical to implement within the current framework of the process under investigation. It wouldn't be a good solution if, for example, people had difficulty understanding how to implement it, so keep your solution as simple as possible. If the solution concerns a work method change, it must be worded in simple terms and then implemented with sufficient training that it leaves no doubt as to what must be done.

Timing is very important, so we don't want a solution that takes days or weeks to implement. The solution needs to be implemented as soon as possible, so that the performance improves as quickly as possible.

We always want our solution to be both effective in dealing with the problem and cost effective. The solution must, first, return the process to a good performance level, while at the same time it must not be too expensive to implement. Fortunately, many solutions don't require much of an investment.

8.3 CHANGE-RELATED PROBLEM SOLUTIONS

If the problem you are trying to solve was found to be the result of a change (i.e., change-related), then the solution should be really quite simple for you. Doesn't it make sense that if the change that created the problem or change in performance in the first place is simply reversed, then the performance should return to where it was before the change? Of course that is completely dependent upon whether you correctly assessed the problem in the first place.

8.4 LAUNCH-RELATED PROBLEM SOLUTIONS

But what about the problem that was not the result of a change (launch-related problem)? Developing a solution for a launch-related problem requires more creativity and a more in-depth review of alternatives. If the solution involves a change in the way a process works, then we must consider all the possible alternative effects that might result from the change. We must look into the future and evaluate all possible outcomes before the change is made.

If there is a defect-free configuration to compare the problem process to, then it simply becomes a matter of finding the distinctions or differences between where or when you have the problem compared to when or where you don't. If the defect-free configuration is a comparison of operators, then the solution will involve imitating the correct work method. If the problem is centered on machines, then the solution will involve finding the differences related to the setup of the machine. When the defect-free configuration is a period of time, such as an hour or day when you have the problem compared to when you don't, then the solution is a bit more difficult. This implies that there is a systemic factor at work that is time based, so the solution will come from determining what is different when the problem exists compared to when the problem doesn't exist.

8.5 HYBRID PROBLEM SOLUTIONS

Hybrid problems, you will recall, are those that combine the elements of both a change- and launch-related problem, so the solutions are logically a combination of both. There is no simple formula for determining a solution, but my suggestion is simple: Take care of reversing the change first and then attack the rest. Just follow the advice I gave you for both the change-related and launch-related problem solutions and good luck.

In the case of the split inner liner, what are the possible negative effects of applying less cement? The cement is intended to create a medium for products to adhere to as the tank-build process progresses, so we must be sure that enough cement is applied but not too much. We certainly don't want to trade one problem for another. So, the team worked on a method to actually measure the thickness of the cement and a visual method to review the tank for completeness of coverage by creating a visual work method with photos of what a "good" tank looked like after application of the cement. The team considered the possible negative outcomes of the change and developed methods to minimize the probability of occurrence of the problem.

8.6 TEST AND SELECT THE BEST SOLUTION

Once again, if the cause of the problem was linked to a known change in the process, then the list of possible solutions will normally be a single entry (assuming only one change had been made to create the problem), with that being to reverse the change. But even though the list might only include one solution, it is still important to make the reversal and then monitor the results just to be sure that the change actually was the root cause.

In the case of multiple, potential solutions, the team must select the "best" solution with respect to complexity, cost, and other factors required to make the change. In the case of the split inner liners, the team had to develop a solution that was robust enough to prevent a recurrence of the problem, and so too must you do the same. Good, effective solutions must be robust enough to weather potential storms that might arise later.

The split inner liner team came up with a solution that considered how to ensure that if the operators followed the new work method, which included thickness measurements of the cement and photos of a tank, with the correct amount of cement on it, then the probability of having split inner liners would be minimized. Now let's look at how best to implement a solution to a problem.

8.7 IMPLEMENT THE BEST SOLUTION

After the solution has been tested, there are several other things that must occur. Communication of the solution to everyone who needs to know is absolutely imperative if the solution is going to be lasting. If it is an operator-controllable solution, doesn't it make sense that the operators completely understand what is to be done differently? But in addition to making sure the appropriate people understand what has to be done, it is always good practice to explain why it has to be done. Most human beings don't like to be told what to do. But, if what has to be done is accompanied with the logic and reasoning behind it, they will usually execute the change without question.

In our case study, it was imperative that the cement operators completely understood the rationale behind the new work method. By explaining why the change was important and making the operators a part of the development of the new work method, the probability of success was high. The team created and implemented a new, visual work method that included photos of the current operators applying the cement using the proper method. By doing this, the operators, in effect, "owned" the solution.

The results of this team's efforts were quite dramatic. This team took on a problem that had been in existence for years and eliminated it as a major problem. The team's success metric proved to everyone that their efforts had paid off. Figure 8.1 is the run chart that the team put in place as its

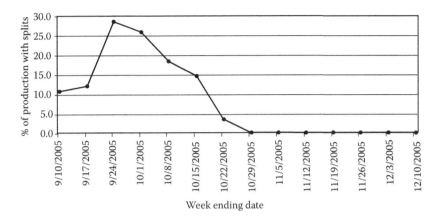

FIGURE 8.1
Run chart of percent of production with inner liner splits by week.

success metric, and as you can see, the problem that had been around for years was no longer a problem. The impact of this achievement was significant, because it not only reduced the daily rework for this defect by eight hours, but it also improved the cycle time of the tanks. This repair took eight hours to fix, but it also had to sit overnight before it could move to the next production step.

Because the team had followed a structured and systematic approach to this problem, success was achieved. But the team knew that its work wasn't quite done yet. Whenever a solution is implemented, it is absolutely essential that a control of some kind is developed and implemented along with the solution. As a matter of fact, no solution is really complete without a control to monitor the performance of the process. We'll discuss this in the next chapter.

9

Implement, Document, and Celebrate

Control your destiny, or somebody else will.

Jack Welch

9.1 SELECT AND IMPLEMENT CONTROLS

No problem-solving event should ever be considered complete until some kind of safeguard is put in place to minimize the probability of a recurrence of the problem. Wouldn't it be a shame after all of the work a team did to determine the root cause of a problem and then implemented a solution that some kind of control of the factor that caused the problem wasn't implemented, and the problem came back into the process. It is important to remember that the purpose of a control is to give an advanced warning that something may be wrong before it is actually wrong. For example, diabetics routinely monitor their blood sugar levels to make sure that the level of their blood sugar stays within an acceptable range. They do this to avoid damaging their vital organs.

By far and away the best type of control is *mistake-proofing* or what the Japanese call a *poka yoke*. Mistake-proofing involves the installation of a sensing or control device within the process that will prevent errors from being made. The advantage of these devices is that defects are prevented, rather than detected. A poka yoke is based upon the premise that 100 percent inspection can be successfully achieved if done by a nonhuman device, rather than by a human who has been proven to not catch all errors. Fail-safe devices can be used effectively to prevent such things as the incorrect positioning of parts or the omission of parts. Unfortunately, sometimes due to the nature of the measurement or because it is cost prohibitive, not all processes are capable of utilizing a fail-safe device. But there are other alternatives.

If it is not possible to implement a fail-safe device, then a manual measurement and a control chart is the second choice. Because the control chart is based upon the normal statistical variability of the process, data is collected and control limits are calculated for the process parameter or product characteristic. Control chart theory states that as long as the measured or calculated data point falls within these limits and the process has been deemed capable, then we are reasonably sure that defects will be caught. The only problem with these type controls is that they are based upon samples, rather than 100 percent inspection.

A control chart is simply a run chart with control limit lines equally spaced from the process average. There are many different varieties of control charts, but in my opinion, the most effective is the x-bar and R chart. This chart simultaneously monitors the location of the process parameter, or product characteristic being measured, relative to the historical average of the process and the amount of variation present. If the calculated average and range remain within predetermined limits, then the process is said to be "in control" and is permitted to continue running. If the process goes outside these control limits, then the process is said to be "out of control" and is stopped while corrective action is taken.

There are many excellent reference books on control charts that summarize other rules that dictate whether a process is out of control, so I suggest you do a Google search to learn more about them.

Figure 9.1 is an example of a control chart that one of my teams developed to control product coming off of a shear machine. The product being controlled with this control chart was a long rectangular piece of metal that not only had to be a certain width but also had to be parallel along the entire length of it. The x-bar (i.e., average) portion of the chart was used to control the width of the rectangle, and the R (i.e., range) portion was used to control its side-to-side parallelism. This chart proved to be a very effective method of control for a problem that had been "fixed" many times in the past. As you can see, the procedure for collecting and recording data is located in the box at the far right side of the chart. Directly beneath the procedure are "rules of action" that define out-of-control conditions and actions the operator should take if or when the process actually goes out of control.

The third, and least attractive, alternative is an audit of the process. Audits are intended to be a review of a procedure or process or system

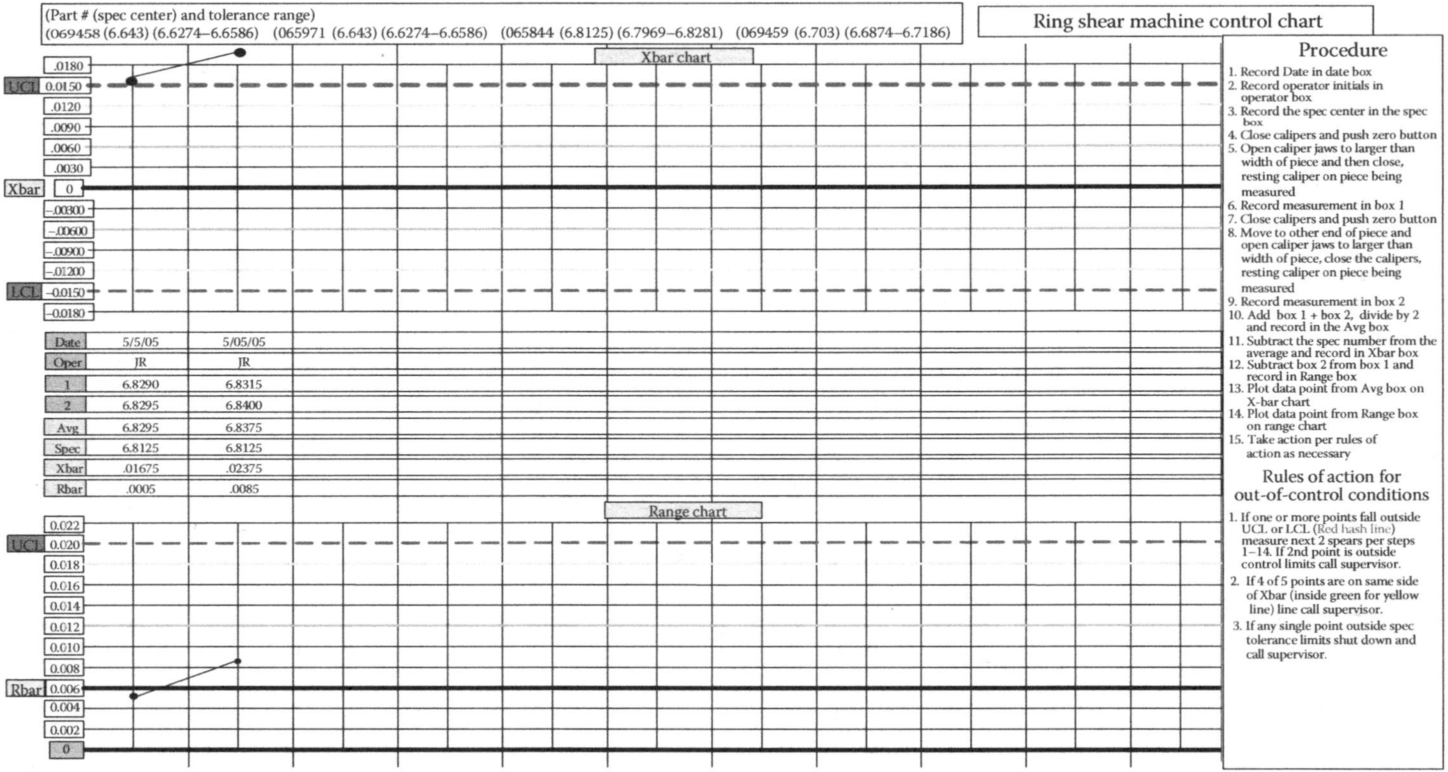

Ring shear machine control chart

(Part # (spec center) and tolerance range)

(069458 (6.643) (6.643) (6.6274–6.6586) (065971 (6.643) (6.6274–6.6586) (065844 (6.8125) (6.7969–6.8281) (069459 (6.703) (6.6874–6.7186)

Xbar chart

Range chart

Procedure

1. Record Date in date box
2. Record operator initials in operator box
3. Record the spec center in the spec box
4. Close calipers and push zero button
5. Open caliper jaws to larger than width of piece and then close, resting caliper on piece being measured
6. Record measurement in box 1
7. Close calipers and push zero button
8. Move to other end of piece and open caliper jaws to larger than width of piece, close the calipers, resting caliper on piece being measured
9. Record measurement in box 2
10. Add box 1 + box 2, divide by 2 and record in the Avg box
11. Subtract the spec number from the average and record in Xbar box
12. Subtract box 2 from box 1 and record in Range box
13. Plot data point from Avg box on X-bar chart
14. Plot data point from Range box on range chart
15. Take action per rules of action as necessary

Rules of action for out-of-control conditions

1. If one or more points fall outside UCL or LCL (Red hash line) measure next 2 spears per steps 1–14. If 2nd point is outside control limits call supervisor.
2. If 4 of 5 points are on same side of Xbar (inside green for yellow line) line call supervisor.
3. If any single point outside spec tolerance limits shut down and call supervisor.

Date	5/5/05	5/05/05		
Oper	JR	JR		
	1	6.8290	6.8315	
	2	6.8295	6.8400	
Avg	6.8295	6.8375		
Spec	6.8125	6.8125		
Xbar	.01675	.02375		
Rbar	.0005	.0085		

UCL 0.0150
.0120
.0090
.0060
.0030
Xbar 0
-.0030
-.0060
-.0090
-.0120
LCL -.0150
-.0180
.0180

UCL 0.022
0.020
0.018
0.016
0.014
0.012
0.010
0.008
Rbar 0.006
0.004
0.002
0

FIGURE 9.1
Control chart of ring shear machine.

to determine if the person performing the work is doing so according to instructions. Audits can work well, as long as the subject of the audit is well defined and the auditor knows exactly what to look for. The problem is that audits are somewhat subjective and have a tendency to evolve over time.

Our split inner liner team members were forced to choose this alternative. They knew now that excessive application of cement was the cause of split inner liners and updated the work method to include photos of a "good" tank. They also added written instructions on how best to apply the cement. The control that the team selected was to, on a weekly basis, monitor the work methods of the cement operators for compliance to the new method. Process audits can be effective if done correctly, but any time there is the option of using either a fail-safe device or a control chart, we should always choose one of these as our control tool.

The key to effective audits is a complete definition of what the auditor is looking for as the process is reviewed. My recommendation here is that the team develop a checklist of items that are important. Since the team knew how important the correct application of cement was to the elimination of inner liner splits, its checklist focus was on this.

The checklist contained a section for application method that attempted to quantify the number of times the operator's mop was dipped into the solvent per tank side; the number and length of strokes of the mop on each side of the tank; the number of times the operator applied cement to the same location; the number of passes over the joint area; the pressure exerted on the mops by the operator; and the direction of application of the cement for each layer. The team believed that if the cement operators performed the work method to a prescribed work method that the incidence of split liners would be significantly reduced or eliminated.

9.2 DOCUMENT YOUR SUCCESS

One final and important activity to complete is to document your success. Documenting how your team successfully solved the problem does several things for the organization. First, it reinforces that the use of a structured and systematic approach to problems really does work. Second, your report is there for future problem-solving teams to follow as a roadmap. Third, if the problem you have solved should ever return (God forbid!), then your team's report is available as a ready reference.

The actual report does not have to be lengthy. In fact, each of the first sixteen steps could serve as the format for the report. I always recommend to companies that they should start a file of "Best Practices," which is simply a collection of solved problems, and your report belongs in this file for future generations of problem solvers.

9.3 CELEBRATE YOUR SUCCESS

The culmination of a successful problem-solving event should always be recognized and celebrated. After all, the team was able to come together as a group, follow a systematic and structured process, and end a problem that was impacting the business. I always end a successful event with doughnuts or some other form of recognition for a job well done, and you should too.

10

Failing at Problem Solving

The range of what we think and do is limited by what we fail to notice. And because we fail to notice that we fail to notice, there is little we can do to change, until we notice how failing to notice shapes our thoughts and deeds.

Ronald Laing

Even though a team might be conscientious and diligent in following the structured approach I have just presented, not all problems get solved the first time through for a variety of reasons. Kepner and Tregoe remind us that it is important to remember that you may fail [1]. If you do fail, then Kepner and Tregoe tell us that there are two primary reasons:

1. The team has insufficient identification of key distinctions and changes.
2. The team has allowed assumptions to distort its judgment during the testing step.

Although the two reasons for failure just listed are the most common, there are other reasons why people fail to solve problems:

1. *Treatment of symptoms instead of the root cause*—Sometimes people get confused and mistake symptoms of the problem for the problem itself. When this happens, temporary, short-term "fixes" or relief actions are applied to problems based on what worked in the past, instead of performing a rigorous problem analysis. It's no different than going to a hospital for severe abdominal pain and rather than determining the source of the pain, the doctor gives you pain pills. The pain medication might give you relief, but the problem is still

there when the effects of the medication (i.e., short-term fix) subside. Based on my experience, treating symptoms rather than finding and eliminating the root cause is a very common occurrence when people are trying to solve problems.

2. *People lack the basic skills necessary for problem solving*—Because many people don't understand the nature of problems, and because they have never really had any formal training in problem analysis, they tend to apply the "change something and see what happens" approach. All this does is complicate the situation, because you lose track of changes and probably worsen the problem. This lack of basic skills is one of the most significant reasons or causes of failed problem-solving initiatives. It's not your fault, since you have probably never been provided any form of effective problem-solving training. Many of you might have received training on specific tools or techniques, like cause-and-effect diagrams or Pareto charts, or maybe even trend charts. But how many of you have learned how and when to use these tools to define a problem, or search for a change, or identify a defect-free configuration, or clarify a distinction? Solving problems requires a systematic approach, and it's my bet many of you have never had this kind of training.

3. *Failure to look at problems holistically*—Many times people only focus on the symptoms of the problem and fail to look at the causal mechanism that created the conditions for the problem to occur. Remember, we are looking for cause-and-effect relationships here. I absolutely agree with Kepner and Tregoe in this aspect, but again, it all comes down to the level of problem-solving training people have received.

4. *Failure to involve the right people*—Problem analysis enables people to work together as a team so as to pool their information. Because many problems are complex, it is difficult, if not impossible, for one person to have all of the knowledge and information needed to be able to solve the problem. Operating in a vacuum not only slows the problem-solving process, it limits the available scope of knowledge, setting up the potential to overlook key bits of information.

5. *Failure to use a structured and systematic approach*—The number one cause for failure to solve problems is the failure to follow a logical and systematic process. When problem-solving teams don't follow a systematic approach, they have a tendency to wander aimlessly, and usually problems do not get solved. It is only through being disciplined enough to use a structured approach that most problems

actually get solved. Although this, again, is a training issue, the reality is that the fault lies with the leader of the organization. The leader must set expectations that structured approaches to problem solving will be used.

6. *Failure to define or understand the real problem*—Defining the problem is absolutely a critical first step in resolving the problem. Without the focus provided by the problem definition, everyone is not properly focused and aligned. Having the entire team aligned is critical to the success of the team. Otherwise people will go off in different directions and the team will most likely fail.

7. *No support or expectations from leadership*—Support and expectations from the leadership in any organization are not only important, but they are critical pieces of the problem-solving pie. If the problem solvers do not get the support they need, and if the expectation of leadership isn't to use a structured approach to solving problems, then, quite simply, problems won't get solved effectively.

11

A Message for Leadership

One of the tests of leadership is the ability to recognize a problem before it becomes an emergency.

Arnold Glasgow

11.1 THE RESPONSIBILITY OF THE LEADER

I once had a vice president of operations for a company ask me what he needed to do to get his people to use a structured approach to problem solving. He had brought in consultants in the past, but his staff continued to be reactive and out of control as it pertains to solving problems. My answer to him was swift and simple. I told him that since he was the leader of the organization, it was up to him to force this behavioral change. Not change by brute force, but rather by setting the appropriate expectations and by setting the right example. I told him that if the leader of an organization doesn't expect, be adamant about, and personally use a structured approach to solving problems, then why should he expect anything different from the rest of his organization? This VP assured me that he did expect this to happen, but he admitted that he did not use it himself.

I prepared a list of questions for him to ask of his people each time they were presenting a problem to him. If they did not have an appropriate answer for the question asked, then the VP was to instruct them to go get the answers and come back to him when they did. Here are the questions I gave him and, where appropriate, the tool to use.

10 Questions from a Leader on Problem Solving

1. What is the problem? (Specifically describe the problem.)
2. Where is the problem occurring? (Where is it in the plant and where is it on the object?)
3. When is the problem occurring? (When did it start and when does it recur? Run chart.)
4. Who has the problem? (Is it one operator or multiple operators? Pareto chart.)
5. What is the scope of the problem? (How many product types have the problem? Or how many machines have the problem?)
6. What is the trend? (Is the problem increasing, decreasing, or remaining constant? Trend or run chart.)
7. What is your problem statement? (Incorporates all of the above responses.)
8. Is it a change-related problem? A launch problem (distinctions)? Or a hybrid problem (a combination of a change and a launch problem)?
9. Have you formed a team? (Is it a diverse group, including at least one operator and one nonproduction member?)
10. When can I expect a solution to the problem?

Soon after this VP began to use these questions on a regular basis, a noticeable change in his and his management team's approach to problems became obvious, and so did the results. In his words, "Problems were actually getting solved!" The leader of the organization is the one who sets the tone and expectations for how things get done and how problems are solved. So, if you want your team to use a structured approach, you better expect it and use it first.

People enjoy the euphoria associated with solving a problem, and it has been my experience that they also enjoy using a process that produces successful results. Kepner and Tregoe tell us that regardless of someone's position within an organization, they will actually seek problem-solving opportunities as long as four conditions exist [1]:

1. They must possess the necessary skills required to solve problems. Not having the necessary skill set usually results in people shying away from problem-solving opportunities.

2. They must experience success in using those skills. When anyone is successful, at any venture, the normal human response is to repeat it again and again, and the same can be said for solving problems.
3. They must be recognized and rewarded for successfully solving problems. People like to be told when they are doing a good job, and this is especially true in problem solving.
4. They must not be afraid to fail. When failure occurs, the natural tendency of humans is to avoid the same situation in the future that resulted in failure in the past or present, especially if they are negatively reinforced.

Conversely, people will actively avoid problem-solving opportunities if they lack the proper skills to be successful at problem solving, when they aren't appreciated when they do solve problems, or when they feel threatened by the situation.

It is important to remember that problem solving is a demonstrable skill that can be learned and acquired, and success can be achieved when this skill is exploited and utilized. In order for this to become a reality, however, the right management environment must exist, one that not only supports the use of a structured approach but also provides the necessary training and then sets expectations to use it. Management must reward and recognize success, and when this fails to happen, that is, expecting a structured approach and then rewarding people when it is not used, problem solving will typically grind to a halt.

My message to leadership then is clear. If you want problems solved, then set high expectations. Expect problems to be solved and expect a structured approach to be used. And by the way, set an example by using the same approach yourself. You won't regret it.

11.2 THE CULTURE OF PROBLEM SOLVING

"It is not uncommon at all for people to rush from one crisis to another, leaving behind a trail littered with the carcasses of unsolved or partially solved problems. In many cases, they never really seem to fix problems, but rather they just stop them from getting any worse." Roger Bohn writes in his classic business article "Stop Fighting Fires" [4]: "In business organizations, there are invariably more problems than people have the time to deal with. At best, this leads to situations where minor problems are ignored. At worst, chronic fire fighting consumes an operation's resources. Managers and engineers rush from task to task, not completing one before another interrupts them. Serious problem-solving efforts degenerate into quick-and-dirty patching. Productivity suffers, and managing becomes a constant juggling act of deciding where to allocate overworked people, and which incipient crisis to ignore for the moment." In effect, the culture exhibits classic fire-fighting behaviors.

In my travels throughout the world, I have been fortunate (or maybe I should say unfortunate) enough to see many examples of fire fighting firsthand, and it's not a pretty sight at all. Bohn and his colleague Ramchandran Jaikumar observed fire-fighting behaviors in many manufacturing and new product development settings, and have actually developed a list of "fire-fighting symptoms" to be used as a guide to determine if an organization is a victim of fire fighting [4]. Their claim is that if your organization exhibits three or more of the following symptoms, then you are the victim of fire fighting:

1. *There isn't enough time to solve all the problems.* The number of problems outnumbers the number of problem solvers. (I have seen this one a lot.)
2. *Solutions are incomplete.* Many problems are simply patched and never really solved. That is, the superficial effects (symptoms) are treated, but the root causes are never eliminated. (This is the most common behavior from my travels.)
3. *Problems recur and cascade.* Incomplete or haphazard solutions usually cause old problems to recur and sometimes create new problems. (Tied to symptom 2.)
4. *Urgency supersedes importance.* The "squeaky wheel gets oiled first" syndrome is usually at work. Problem-solving efforts never really continue to fruition, because of constant interruptions, due to fires that must be extinguished. (Usually happens because priorities aren't realized.)
5. *Performance drops.* Because of the ineffective problem solving that always occurs, overall performance usually always drops dramatically. (A natural cause-and-effect relationship.)

6. *Many problems become crises.* Problems smolder until they flare up, often just before a deadline, and then they require heroic efforts to solve. (Thompson's law tells us that Murphy is an optimist.)

11.3 CRISIS AND FAILURE

On this last observation (i.e., many problems become crises), Bohn hypothesized that one reason American factories were more chaotic than Japanese factories was the difference in culture. He wrote, "American managers actually *enjoy* crises; they often get their greatest personal satisfaction, the most recognition, and their biggest rewards from solving crises. Crises are part of what makes work fun. To Japanese managers, however, a crisis is evidence of failure" [4]. I totally concur with Bohn, but I would add that this realization of failure extends beyond just Japanese managers to include organizations (even American) that have developed strong problem-solving cultures. That is, most successful organizations recognize the need to be proactive in their approach to problems and simply won't tolerate chronic crises.

Bohn tells us that fire fighting isn't necessarily disastrous, and while it clearly hampers performance, there are worse alternatives: "Rigid bureaucratic rules can help a company avoid fire fighting altogether, but at the price of almost no problems getting solved. Also, sometimes even a well-managed organization slips into a fire-fighting mode temporarily without creating long-term problems. The danger is that the more intense fire fighting becomes, the more difficult it is to escape from" [4].

But why is it that some companies almost never fight fires, even though they have the same amount of work and the same amount of resources? How is it that these companies are able to avoid the fire-fighting trap? Based upon my experiences (and that of Bohn), it is because of the existence of their strong problem-solving cultures, cultures that are committed to finding root causes and genuine solutions to problems, instead of just patching them with temporary fixes and moving on to new ones. Or as Bohn tells us, "they perform triage." Bohn claims that the key to success for these companies is that they refuse to reward fire fighting. Let me say that again. *They refuse to reward fire fighting!* They insist upon a rigid analysis of the problem, a discovery of the true root cause(s) of the problem, and then and only then, do they implement solutions that work. They don't permit their problem solvers to ride in on white horses and save the day. As a matter of fact, the successful companies either shoot all their white horses, or they put them to pasture.

11.4 TRAFFIC INTENSITY

Bohn introduces what he refers to as *traffic intensity*, or the number of problems relative to the resources devoted to problem solving. Bohn presents the following equation:

$$\text{Traffic intensity} = \frac{(\text{Days to solve}) \times (\text{Number of new problems/day})}{\text{Number of problem solvers}}$$

Traffic intensity increases when there is an increase in the number of problems, more days required to solve the problems, and/or the number of problem solvers available decreases. Conversely, the traffic intensity decreases when the number of problems to be solved and/or the time required to solve problems decreases, and/or as the number of available problem solvers increases. Bohn also tells us that as long as the traffic intensity stays below 80%, the system seems to work well, but when the value nears or exceeds 100%, that is, when there are more problems than can be solved, organizations get into real trouble. The queue lengthens and problem resolution becomes extended. If, for example, three problems arise each day and four problem solvers take an average of two days to solve each problem, then by the end of the third week fifteen problems are waiting in queue. As this queue grows, the problem solvers and their managers feel pressure (i.e., the self-imposed internal pressure of knowing they are behind and external pressure from customers, senior managers, etc.) and the severity of fire fighting increases until the system breaks down.

Problems also bypass the queue because of political reasons, and problem solvers find themselves spending less time actually working on the problem and more time in meetings or preparing documentation in response to irate inquiries. The problem-solving effort becomes less efficient, precisely when the most work needs to get done. In general, problem solvers are dealing with chaos and information overload, but even worse, the problems are not only solved inefficiently but badly as well. "Gut feel" solutions to problems become the norm until finally the system simply shuts down.

11.5 THE EFFECTS OF FIRE FIGHTING

The important lesson Bohn [4] reinforces for us is this: Although structured and systematic problem solving appears to take longer than "gut feel" techniques, in reality the exact opposite is true. Patching not only takes more time than systematic problem solving, it also fails to fix problems. As Bohn points out, "Haphazardly introduced changes raise an even more serious issue: they can easily create new problems elsewhere in the process." With few exceptions, fire fighting and patching are destructive, because solution rates fall and the number of hidden problems increases. Bohn characterizes this phenomenon in Figure 11.1. Here we see the new flow of problems through an organization. Bohn tells us that new problems and opportunities continue entering the organization as before, but now, because of the number of badly solved problems, an invisible queue of unresolved problems emerge and reenter the system in the form of repeat problems, and overloads the system. Now the organization has the new problems that patching has created, the old ones that patching has failed to serve, and the new problems that are normally present. In effect, fire fighting has tripled the opportunity for problems to flow into the organization.

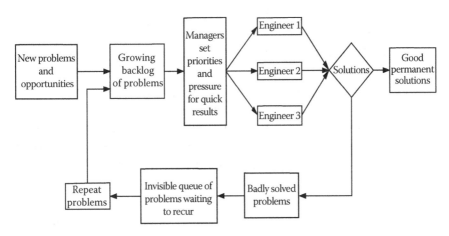

FIGURE 11.1
Flowchart of the effects of fire-fighting syndrome.

The problem solvers' environment becomes increasingly chaotic, because there is less time to study problems the correct way, and in some cases the organization's ability to solve problems collapses completely. And, of course, the performance of the organization rapidly deteriorates. This deterioration then calls for drastic action to be taken, like outsourcing or bringing in a costly massive infusion of outside help.

Earlier I mentioned in passing that patching is unacceptable with few exceptions. Bohn tells us that patching and its superficial solutions are acceptable, if several conditions are met:

1. Patching should improve much of the damage, even though the cause has not been addressed.
2. The patches should be solid enough that they won't break down later.
3. The patch should have a better cost-benefit ratio than other solutions, with the cost, in this case, being the problem solvers' time and not dollars.

11.6 ESCAPING FIRE FIGHTING

So, the obvious question is this: How do some companies escape from, or avoid, the evil clutches of fire fighting while others can't. Like all good problem-solving methodologies, before we can correct or reduce the impact of fire fighting, we really need to understand the underlying causes for it. Again, we turn to Bohn who developed a simple fire-fighting model (see Figure 11.2) that helps us understand the flow of problems through organizations.

Bohn used an example of a factory engineering group in the midst of a new product ramp-up. As problems arise from customer complaints, special orders, quality issues, supplier problems, and so forth, they are sent into a queue until they are assigned to an engineer (it doesn't have to be an engineer) by a manager or a committee. As the engineer finishes his problem, the manager presiding over the queue decides which problems are the most urgent and selects the most qualified engineer to work on it. Because of the nature of problems (i.e., differences in size, shape, complexity, etc.), allocation of problems to problem solvers is not always a simple task. Different people have different knowledge bases, experience levels,

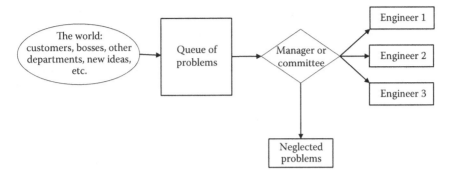

FIGURE 11.2
Flowchart of problems.

and so forth, so matching the right person to the right problem isn't necessarily straightforward.

So, if your organization is mired in fire fighting, what can you do to resolve this condition? Bohn tells us that fire fighting can be eliminated, but it requires a level of commitment that did not exist before the situation escalated to where it is. Bohn suggests that there are primarily three approaches for eliminating fire fighting:

1. Tactical methods
2. Strategic methods
3. Cultural methods

Tactical methods. When the queue of problems becomes overwhelming and the organization is about to collapse, bringing in temporary help is usually a good short-term fix, if they are selected according to their field of expertise.

Another method that can be used effectively to limit the flow of problems to the queue is to do deliberately what will ultimately happen anyway: admit that some problems will not be solved. Bohn tells us that this technique, borrowed from military medicine, controls the queue by regulating entry into it. Instead of letting problems queue up indefinitely, decide whether to commit resources to a problem when it first emerges. (I do not recommend this approach, but I'm told that it works some of the time.)

Strategic methods. This approach to fire fighting typically takes longer to implement than tactical methods, but the long-term pay off is substantial. These methods usually always result in a dramatic increase in the number of problems solved, but the commitment required is much higher. The most obvious of these methods is to *change design strategies*. It should be clear that these days it is generally recognized that the most cost-effective strategy for quality is quality by design. By focusing your engineering group on design issues, the number of product problems dramatically decreases. In addition, design solutions will typically transcend product lines, with the result being improved baseline products.

Along with designing quality into the products, companies should develop more problem solvers. For me, this is the key to success for all organizations. By involving more people in the correct method for root cause analysis, that is, a structured and systematic method, the resource base for problem solving expands and problems are correctly addressed in much shorter time intervals.

Cultural methods. One thing we are sure of in organizations is that change is difficult for some members of the organization. Change requires both a shift in the mind-set of the entire organization and behavioral changes of senior management. The organization's problem-solving culture *must be top down driven, and the expectations of senior and middle leadership must be one that will not accept fire fighting.* Here are some guidelines:

1. *Don't tolerate patching.* I cannot overemphasize this point, but enforcing this requires the support and commitment of management at all levels. If lower-level employees see that patching is no longer acceptable from an organizational perspective, they will no longer do so.
2. *Don't push to meet deadlines at all costs.* One of the root causes of creating a fire-fighting environment is unreasonable and inflexible deadlines. Your organization must give your problem solvers ample time to study the problem, determine potential root cause, study alternative solutions, and time to implement the best solutions under control.
3. *Don't reward fire fighting.* I cannot emphasize enough how critical this is if you want to experience a cultural change. On the other hand, the people that should be rewarded are managers who don't have fires to put out. Those who practice *problem prevention* should be held in the highest esteem and praised and honored for doing so.

12

A Structured Approach to Problem Prevention

Intellectuals solve problems; geniuses prevent them.

Albert Einstein

12.1 AN OUNCE OF PREVENTION

It seems that we spend an inordinate amount of time working on solving problems that already exist, when in reality many of our problems could have been avoided if we had simply taken the time up front to work on preventing them. Fundamentally, prevention involves identifying potential areas of vulnerability and the problems that could occur within these areas, and then developing and implementing actions aimed at either preventing them, or reducing the probability that they will occur, or even lessening their effects in the event that our prevention plans didn't work as we had envisioned they would.

If you think about it, it makes much more sense to tie up resources working on preventing negative performance than it does spending time trying to understand why the negative performance happened in the first place. Being a preventive organization has so many more benefits than being a reactive organization. Just think about how negative performance affects an organization for a moment. Problems create things like scrap and rework, late shipments and missed deliveries, higher inventory levels, and the list goes on. Imagine how things might look in your company or organization if you minimized the number of problems you had by being preventive instead of reactive. Would your job be more stressful or less stressful? Would your customers be more content or less content? Would your market share be shrinking or growing? Being a preventive organization will place your company at a distinct advantage with margins moving in the right direction.

Making changes to processes, systems, and even strategies is commonplace in every organization, but thinking into the future isn't so ordinary. Whenever a change or modification is being contemplated or considered, it is critical to think about the potential negative effects or consequences of the change. Blindly making changes can be disastrous or even catastrophic if the change isn't thought through with respect to potential outcomes, so take the time to look into the future. Prevention is a positive mind-set, with your focus being to create a positive future, minimizing the unexpected. Prevention is being proactive rather than being reactive. As the old adage says, "An ounce of prevention is worth a pound of cure."

12.2 BECOMING PROACTIVE RATHER THAN REACTIVE

In this chapter, we will explore basic ways to prevent problems rather than trying to solve them after they materialize. We will look at ways to stroll into the future, predict what could happen, and then return to the present, developing ways to prevent any potential future problems. We will, in effect, look at ways to take control of the future rather than having the future control us. In doing so, we will demonstrate several tools that can be used to predict what could happen. Since we can never be certain of future events, we will speak in terms of simple probabilities and look at ways to predict the future with a relative degree of certainty. Just always remember that we are attempting to become proactive and positive rather than reactive and negative.

12.3 PROBABILITY AND RISK

Before we begin our discussion on problem prevention, we need to speak just a bit about simple probability and risk analysis. At one time or another, all of us have used a coin flip to make a decision. It's used in football games to determine who kicks off and who receives the football first. With a coin flip, there are only two possible outcomes. The coin will either be a heads or tails, so the probability of guessing right is one out of two, or fifty percent. If you were to flip the coin one hundred times, you would most likely have approximately fifty heads and fifty tails.

In cards, if we want to know the probability of randomly selecting a four of any suit, for example, we know that there are fifty-two cards in a deck and four of each type card, so the odds of drawing a four randomly from a deck of cards is one in thirteen. A bit more complicated than a simple coin flip but still easy to understand. If we were to calculate the odds of drawing a four of hearts, then the odds would be one in fifty-two. And if you play the lottery, you already know by the number of nonpaying tickets that the odds are astronomical against you selecting the right numbers. In each of these examples, you are able to calculate the odds of winning.

Calculating probabilities is another way of measuring risk, and we all know that every decision involves a certain amount of risk. When we operate in a preventive environment, we are attempting to minimize this risk. The difference between solving a problem and preventing a problem is simply one of timing. In problem solving we are in a reactive mode, after the fact, trying to determine why something *did happen*. In problem prevention, we are in a proactive mode, trying to determine what *could happen*. Unlike games of chance, like the coin flip or the card draw, trying to predict or estimate the odds of something specific happening requires that we use primarily our past experience or maybe some data we have collected in a similar experience.

12.4 THE PROBLEM PREVENTION ROADMAP

Like problem solving, there are a series of steps, or a roadmap, that can be followed to successfully analyze and hopefully prevent future potential problems. Figure 12.1 is such a roadmap. The *Problem Prevention Roadmap* contains six major sections and a total of seventeen individual steps. If you will diligently follow this roadmap, I am convinced that you will significantly improve your chances of becoming a more proactive organization, anticipating problems rather than reacting to them. In the next six chapters I will present the roadmap and its six major segments:

1. Defining the high risk or vulnerable areas of your organization
2. Defining the potential problems, failure modes, and their effects

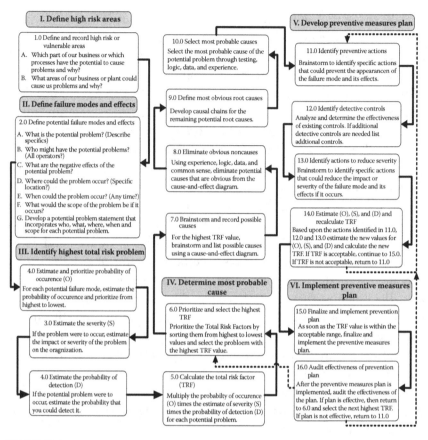

FIGURE 12.1
Problem Prevention Roadmap.

3. Identifying the highest total risk problems
4. Determining the most probable cause of the highest risk problem
5. Developing a preventive measures plan
6. Implementing the preventive measures plan

Each of these segments includes individual actions that are focused solely on future potential events. If you execute these actions, you will either (1) prevent the problem totally, (2) increase the probability that if the problem does occur you will be able to detect it before any damage is done, or (3) minimize the impact or severity of the problem if it does occur. This roadmap can be used to evaluate proposed changes, equipment installations, personnel policy changes, and virtually anything that involves a future activity. Now let's look at each of the major segments and action steps more closely.

These seventeen individual action steps will facilitate your efforts to attempt to control your own future and destiny. Each of these seventeen actions requires that we reach deep into our experiences, bag of tools, techniques, and personality traits in a proactive manner.

Before we look at each of these six major segments and seventeen action steps more closely, you need to understand one simple fact. In general, people have a hang-up with the future. That is to say, typically, we are so caught up in the chaos of problems in the present and leftover problems from the past that we rarely take the time to look into the future. People want and need to be future oriented, to be proactive, but the pressures of problems already upon us typically preclude this from happening.

13

Defining High-Risk Areas

Living at risk is jumping off the cliff and building your wings on the way down.

Ray Bradbury

13.1 IDENTIFY THE HIGH RISK OR VULNERABLE AREAS OF YOUR ORGANIZATION

Our first action toward our look into the future starts with an identification of areas within our organization or plant or a specific process that could be at risk or vulnerable. These are areas that could be potential show-stoppers for your organization. They can be specific processes, systems, or even strategies that could negatively impact the long-term viability and profitability of your company or facility. In this activity you are asking questions like, Which part of our business or plant has the potential to go awry and cause us problems and why? or What areas in our business or plant could cause us problems in the future and why? The questions need to be open-ended and require more than just a yes or no response. Remember, we are trying to identify areas of high risk.

Examples of high-risk areas could be something like having a single supplier of raw materials or parts, or maybe maintenance services if you contract out your maintenance. Other typical examples might be hourly labor or potential labor contract disputes, the pricing of your products, your research and development organization, your customers, or any other part of your business or plant. Remember, in this step, we are only trying to define and identify areas within the business that could go wrong and not the actual potential problems. That will come next.

Identification of these high-risk areas, in many cases, involves critically and openly looking at future strategies, plans, or proposed changes, and then trying to imagine what could go wrong if the plan or change wasn't successful. A good technique is to first develop a step-by-step project management plan, and then review each important step or milestone for what could go wrong. We should be especially critical of anything that the organization has never done before or things outside the current core competency. If there is a time constraint involved, it is even more important to focus on that activity. Every plan or strategy contains linchpins or critical factors that control the eventual success or failure of any project. Linchpins are the glue that holds plans together, and if they are removed, the plans could come crashing down, so you should focus on them.

Now that you have created your list of areas of vulnerability, it's time to select the one (or two) that will have the biggest impact on the organization. Impact, in this case, could be things like loss of revenue, loss of jobs, vulnerability to lawsuits, loss of capacity, and inability to supply goods and services.

In this step, we are looking at potential problems from ten thousand feet. That is, we are using our intuition and logic to whittle our list to a manageable size of, say, two or three potential problems. One simple way to do this is to consider the following two elements:

1. The chances of the event going wrong
2. The overall negative impact on the organization

TABLE 13.1

Chances of Occurring versus Consequences Table

Occurrence and Consequences Ratings				
		Consequences		
		Low	Medium	High
Chances of Occurring	Low	Green zone	Green zone	Yellow zone
	Medium	Green zone	Yellow zone	Red zone
	High	Yellow zone	Red zone	Red zone

Table 13.1 is a simple tool that any organization can use to select the right area of vulnerability. We are considering the potential negative consequences facing the organization and the chances of the negative event actually happening. Each potential problem or negative event is rated as low, medium, or high, for both *occurrence* and *consequences,* and placed directly into the appropriate box within the table. As you might have speculated, any potential negative event or proposed project that falls within a red box should be selected. Conversely, any event or area that falls within a green block should be crossed off the list. The yellow blocks are borderline and represent those events that may or may not be included on your final list.

Once your most important areas of vulnerability have been defined and consensus has been achieved, it is now time to define the potential problems, failure modes, and potential negative effects that could occur in these areas.

14

Defining Problems, Failure Modes, and Effects

Again and again, the impossible decision is solved when we see that the problem is only a tough decision waiting to be made.

Dr. Robert Schuller

14.1 IDENTIFY POTENTIAL PROBLEMS, FAILURE MODES, AND EFFECTS IN HIGH-RISK AREAS

A *failure mode* is defined as the way(s) that a system or subsystem could *fail to perform its intended function*(s). *Effects*, on the other hand, are the *consequences* that will take place as a result of a failure mode.

Once you have identified the areas of high risk, it is time to brainstorm specific problems or failures that could occur. In order for this activity to be effective, you must specify the *who, what, where, when,* and *scope* of potential problems. Now is the time to be as specific as possible, so try to stay away from broad generalizations. The more detailed the description, the more specific the action plan will be later. Incidentally, doesn't the list of questions that must be answered look familiar? These are the same type of questions you were asking when you were trying to define an existing problem. The difference here is one of timing. Instead of working to solve an existing problem, you are working to prevent a potential problem, so remember this as you go through the steps.

In this first step, suppose you have identified a sole supplier of a product as a vulnerable area or area at risk. Ask yourself what problems could emerge by having a single-source supplier. The answer to what in this case might be the inability of the supplier to ship specific parts or materials without adequate advanced notification. Since you have no backup supplier, a delayed shipment of parts or a materials shortage could last for some time. The answer to where is the location of the supplier and where in your production plant you might be affected. The answer to when would be an alarming, "At any time in the future!" The scope of the problem would be dependent upon how many of your own products require parts or materials from the supplier in question. Any part or material received from that supplier used in any of your product lines could be at risk.

Another example might be that you are a highly automated producer of products and you have no internal maintenance of your own. If you are contracting with an outside group to maintain the equipment, then you could be vulnerable. Your potential problem in this case is extended periods of downtime which, in turn, could cause your products to be late to your customers. In both of these examples we have identified a linchpin that could put your organization at risk. Remember, in the first two steps you are only searching for areas of your organization that could be at risk or vulnerable and specific problems that might occur, not the causes. That will come later.

15

Identifying the Highest Total Risk Problem

Progress always involves risk. You can't steal second base and keep your foot on first.

Frederick Wilcox

15.1 ESTIMATE THE PROBABILITY OF OCCURRENCE FOR EACH PROBLEM

Whenever you are asked to "estimate" something, you typically rely on similar past experiences that might fit into a specific condition or situation. Hopefully you may also be able to utilize data, in some form, to help you predict a potential problem. By knowing how some similar problem reacted, you usually go with your best estimate. For example, if you are comparing a similar defect, then use the same defect rate. But what if you don't have data or even a past experience that fits this situation? What do you do then? As appalling as this may sound to you, sometimes you just have to go with your gut feel, but when you do make certain that you err on the conservative side. If you make a mistake, what's the worst thing that could happen to you? You would have overestimated the probability and that's all, with no damage done!

So, the question is, how do you estimate the probability that a particular event will take place? Here is a very simple, uncomplicated, and straightforward way to estimate simple probabilities. Using a scale of 1 to 10, consider each problem by itself, and then rate each problem as to how certain or uncertain you are that it will occur. A rating of 10 would mean that you are 100% confident that the problem will occur under certain conditions. A rating of 1, on the other hand, might denote or imply that there is no possibility the problem will occur. The numbers between 1 and 10 will be used to estimate how certain or uncertain you are, but remember, be conservative. Logically, if you have no idea whether the problem will occur, then you might rate the problem as a 5.

Table 15.1, of unknown origin, is frequently used in the auto industry to estimate the probability of occurrence. The table contains three columns, and each column provides a different piece of information that will help you with your estimate. The first column is the actual numerical ranking from 10 to 1. The second column is an actual probability value, and the third column is a description that corresponds to the level of probability.

A ranking of 10 suggests that the failure mode is almost certain to occur, whereas 1 specifies that failure is almost an impossibility. The other numbers between 10 and 1 have discrete probabilities depending upon your beliefs, experiences from the past, and level of confidence. The true value of a table like this is that if you aren't particularly comfortable or confident that you can accurately estimate the numerical probability of the failure, then you can still use the descriptive column to estimate and assign a ranking. In any event, it's important that you contemplate your own personal experiences and those of your team, and then discuss them thoroughly before assigning a ranking number.

TABLE 15.1

Probability of Occurrence versus Probability of Failure

Ranking	Probability of Occurrence (O)	Probability of Failure
10	≥1 in 2	Almost certain to occur
9	1 in 3	Very high chance of occurring
8	1 in 8	High chance of occurring
7	1 in 20	Moderately high chance of occurring
6	1 in 80	Medium chance of occurring
5	1 in 400	Low chance of occurring
4	1 in 2000	Slight chance of occurring
3	1 in 15,000	Very slight chance of occurring
2	1 in 150,000	Remote chance of occurring
1	1 in 1,500,000	Almost impossible to occur

15.2 ESTIMATE THE POTENTIAL SEVERITY OF THE PROBLEM

Once again, you are asked to estimate something, but this time it isn't a probability, it's an estimate of how severe, acute, or serious the problem might be if it were to occur. There are numerous references on particular ways to estimate severity, but again, let's keep it simple. I have found that, once again, a simple 1 to 10 rating scale is the most uncomplicated way to estimate severity. Although I am not certain of the origin of Table 15.2, I find it, or a variation of it, to be most helpful when assigning a severity ranking. You will notice from the descriptions in the table, that it was probably developed somewhere within the auto industry, but it would be relatively simple for you to modify it to meet your needs in your industry.

In this table, we see columns for ranking the verbal interpretation of severity and severity criteria. A ranking of 10, for example, is labeled as "hazardous," and the criteria include things like "without warning,"

TABLE 15.2

Severity and Severity Criteria

Ranking	Severity (S)	Severity Criteria
10	Hazardous	Hazardous effect without warning. Safety related. Regulatory noncompliant.
9	Serious	Potential hazardous effect. Able to stop without mishap. Regulatory compliance in jeopardy.
8	Extreme	Item inoperable but safe. Customer very dissatisfied.
7	Major	Performance severely affected but functional and safe. Customer dissatisfied.
6	Significant	Performance degraded but operable and safe. Nonvital part inoperable. Customer experiences discomfort.
5	Moderate	Performance moderately affected. Fault on nonvital part requires repair. Customer experiences some dissatisfaction.
4	Minor	Minor effect on performance. Fault does not require repair. Nonvital fault always noticed. Customer experiences minor nuisance.
3	Slight	Slight effect on performance. Nonvital fault notice most of the time. Customer is slightly annoyed.
2	Very slight	Very slight effect on performance. Nonvital fault may be noticed. Customer is not annoyed.
1	None	No effect

"safety," and "regulatory noncompliance." On the other end of the scale, a ranking of 1 means that it is totally safe, with no effects expected or anticipated. The numbers between 10 and 1 are simply progressive changes in severity. As with the probability of occurrence table, you should use past, similar experiences, and discuss the ranking with your team before you make the final ranking selection.

15.3 ESTIMATE THE PROBABILITY OF DETECTION

Omitted from many books and articles on the subject of potential problems is the concept of being able to detect the problem or failure either before or immediately after it occurs. In my mind, this is a crucial and essential part of potential problem analysis, and I am at a loss as to why it isn't discussed. The first point to contemplate when considering how we might be able to detect a failure is to look at and consider the current controls that are in place. The current controls (either design or process) are the methods or testing already in place that notify or alert us that the cause of the failure mode could be present. Once we have identified the controls, we must turn our attention to evaluating their effectiveness and make a determination as to whether we must add additional controls. Remember, the important step here is that we want to be able to recognize the occurrence of the failure. If we aren't comfortable with the current controls, then we must develop and add additional controls that improve the probability of detection. Each of these controls should be assessed on their ability to detect the presence of the failure modes.

Table 15.3, like the tables for occurrence and severity, provides a grading of the probability of detection of the presence of the effects of the failure mode. The scale is the same 1 to 10 ranking, but this time, the order is reversed from the way you might expect. That is, the ranking of 10, in this case, is interpreted as meaning that we are certain that the controls in place will not to detect the effects of the potential failure mode. Conversely, a ranking of 1 means that we are almost certain that the controls in place will detect the effects of the potential failure mode. This is done so because it would be very risky if we were not able to detect the presence of the failure.

TABLE 15.3

Probability of Detection

Ranking	Detection (D)	Likelihood of Detection by Design Control
10	Absolute uncertainty	No controls in place to detect the presence of the effects of the potential failure mode.
9	Very remote	Very remote chance that the controls in place will detect the presence of the effects of the potential failure mode.
8	Remote	Remote chance that the controls in place will detect the presence of the effects of the potential failure mode.
7	Very low	Very low chance that the controls in place will detect the presence of the effects of the potential failure mode.
6	Low	Low chance that the controls in place will detect the presence of the effects of the potential failure mode.
5	Moderate	Moderate chance that the controls in place will detect the presence of the effects of the potential failure mode.
4	Moderately high	Moderately high chance that the controls in place will detect the presence of the effects of the potential failure mode.
3	High	High chance that the controls in place will detect the presence of the effects of the potential failure mode.
2	Very high	Very high chance that the controls in place will detect the presence of the effects of the potential failure mode.
1	Almost certain	Almost certain that the controls in place will detect the presence of the effects of the potential failure mode.

15.4 CALCULATE AND PRIORITIZE THE TOTAL RISK FACTOR FOR EACH PROBLEM

The next step in this process is to calculate what I refer to as the *total risk factor* (TRF) for each of the potential failure modes. The total risk factor is simply the product of the occurrence (O), severity (S), and detection (D) rankings. The formula then for the total risk factor is

$$TRF = O \times S \times D$$

For example, suppose our ranking for occurrence was 9, our severity ranking was 5, and our detection ranking was 10. The total risk factor would be 9 times 5 times 10 or 450.

We then calculate and prioritize each of the calculated TRF values by arranging them in order from highest to lowest. If you were wondering why I recommend a scale of 1 to 10 for ranking the risk factors (i.e., occurrence, severity, and detection), as opposed to say a scale of 1 to 5, the answer is really quite simple. By using the larger range of numbers (i.e., 1 to 10), there will be a wider range of TRF values making it easier to differentiate or separate the really important potential failure modes from the less important. By doing this, we will facilitate their prioritization.

With multiple potential failure modes, how do you know which TRF values to act upon first? Clearly, we want to be able to develop preventive action plans for the most important potential problems first. So, we need some way of differentiating or discriminating the truly important ones, from the less important ones. It would make little sense to act upon less important areas of risk before we acted on obvious ones. Table 15.4 contains a guide, if you will, that should assist you. Like the other tables for estimation of risk factors, this table originated in the auto industry.

The interpretation of this table is pretty straightforward. All values of TRF that fall above 700 must be acted upon first. My recommendation is that any value of 500 or greater should be considered a candidate for inclusion in the preventive action plan. Even though you will most likely have multiple potential problems, don't be surprised if there are one or two TRF values that are conspicuous, or more prominent, than all the others. These are the ones that you will act on first.

TABLE 15.4

Impact versus Action

TRF Value	Impact	Action
1–10	Minor impact/risk	Minor design changes, process improvements, or increased controls are needed.
11–125	Moderate impact/risk	Moderate design changes, process improvements, or increased controls are needed.
125–700	Major impact/risk	Major design changes, process improvements, and 100% inspection are needed. Production may have to be stopped.
>700	Catastrophic impact/risk	If in production, stop and redesign product or process, 100% improved inspection, etc., until problem is resolved.

15.5 PRIORITIZE AND SELECT THE PROBLEM WITH THE HIGHEST TOTAL RISK FACTOR

Now that you have calculated total risk factors for all of the potential problems, it is now time to select the highest priority one. The selection process is really quite simple, assuming you have done a good job of accurately estimating your three risk factors (i.e., occurrence, severity, and detection). Simply arrange the TRF values from highest to lowest, and you have the priority order. If you have two TRFs with the same value, I recommend that you select the one that has the highest severity potential, the one that could have the most negative impact on the organization. Some people might disagree with that, but it is my recommendation.

16

Determine the Most Probable Cause

The measure of success is not whether you have a tough problem to deal with, but whether it is the same problem you had last year.

John Foster Dulles

16.1 BRAINSTORM POSSIBLE CAUSES

Once you have identified potential problems, failure modes, and effects, and then prioritized them according to total risk factor (TRF) values, you are now ready to look for potential reasons that could cause the potential problem to actually materialize. The good news is that you already know how to do this. The same tools that are used to develop potential causes for existing problems can be used to cultivate a list of potential causes for potential problems. The cause-and-effect diagram is the preferred tool or technique used to create this list, so the directions provided earlier in this book in Chapter 4 apply here as well. Instead of brainstorming to find potential causes of a present-day problem, we are simply proactively looking into the future at a potential problem and generating a list of potential causes.

16.2 ELIMINATE OBVIOUS NONCAUSES

As I explained earlier in this book, not all of the possible causes listed on the cause-and-effect diagram will survive the testing, logic, scrutiny, experience, and data to keep them on your list of potential causes. Some will become casualties. Eliminating possible causes from the cause-and-effect diagram will only happen as a result of thoroughly analyzing data, uncovering facts, having discussions, and achieving a consensus among team members. Notice I didn't say that to eliminate a possible cause everyone on the team must agree on its removal. We would certainly like that to be the case, but in reality, it doesn't always happen this easily. What can be done when one or two of the team members don't agree with the majority of the team is to agree to rethink the point later if the team fails to solve the problem. We certainly don't ever want to alienate any team member, so my suggestion is to seek an amicable agreement and then move on with the process.

16.3 IDENTIFY THE MOST LIKELY POTENTIAL ROOT CAUSES

Just like the identification of potential root causes of existing problems, we do the same for potential problems. We employ the same tools and techniques used for an existing problem to identify root causes for potential problems. The causal chain is, once again, the best tool for this exercise. Use the same directions as provided in Chapter 4.

Suppose, for example, that we have identified the failure of a major piece of production equipment as the potential problem. We have brainstormed and created a list of potential effects and causes of failure. How do we know which potential cause of failure is the most likely to occur? Some of the potential problem causes can be eliminated through discussion, but invariably we will still be left with a short list. My recommendation is to prioritize the remaining causes as a group by considering things like current failure rates of the equipment and historical information. Based upon this information, rank order the remaining causes and one-by-one create causal chains to arrive at the most likely cause for each one. These are the potential showstoppers.

16.4 SELECT THE MOST PROBABLE CAUSE

The difference between selecting the most probable cause of an existing problem compared to a potential problem that might occur sometime in the future is your ability to perform tests to rule out a potential problem.

We would love to be able to test every potential cause, but in reality, it is not always possible. The elimination of potential problems usually requires the use of logic, reasoning, intuition, and, whenever possible, your past experiences in a similar situation or set of circumstances. Sometimes we will be lucky enough to have had experience with the same kind of problem, but don't count on it. So, for this reason it is absolutely imperative that the team use methodical, logical reasoning when selecting the most probable potential cause of the problem.

Because you are peering into the future, it is sometimes difficult to agree on a single most probable cause, and invariably your team will be left with two or three most probable causes. Although some people will tell you to vote to reach a consensus, I don't like this method. You certainly don't want to take a chance on something that one or two members feel strongly about. If you can't agree on a singular most probable cause, then so be it. In the next step, you will be developing a preventive measures plan, so if you can't agree on one most probable cause, use however many most probable causes and build your plan around all of them. However, I say this with caution. If you have more than three most probable causes, then you must have more discussion.

17

Developing the Preventive
Measures Plan

It is very dangerous to go into eternity with possibilities which one has oneself prevented from becoming realities. A possibility is a hint from God. One must follow it.

Sören Kierkegaard

17.1 A DISCUSSION REGARDING THE PLAN

At the risk of being unnecessarily cautious or even redundant, I want to recapitulate the purpose and value of the preventive measures plan. The plan in its finished form will have three essential component elements or parts. The first part involves identifying specific actions that are intended to prevent the problem and its effects from occurring. The second, and equally important component, is focused on limiting the damage in the event that our preventive actions don't deliver the expected results. The third part of the plan involves the development and use of detective controls that should let us know that the problem is present. All three components are important and integral parts of the preventive measures plan.

17.2 IDENTIFY PREVENTIVE ACTIONS

Creating preventive or deterrent actions for a future, potential root cause is no different than doing the same thing for an existing problem. Your focus so far has been aimed at identifying potential root causes and, hopefully, you have been fortunate enough to have agreed on a single, most probable root cause, but typically this isn't the case. Once you have determined what could cause the future potential problem, you must search for ways to prevent the problem from occurring. This will involve being creative and inventive, and you may or may not be able to test your actions ahead of time to ensure that your actions will prevent or preclude the problem from occurring. I always recommend to teams that they use the causal chains developed earlier to better understand the potential causes of the potential problem. Use these causal chains to identify actions aimed at preventing the problem.

17.3 IDENTIFY ACTIONS TO REDUCE SEVERITY

Once we have identified the most probable cause of the problem and identified preventive actions, we must now turn our attention to the estimated seriousness or severity of the potential failure and its effects. As we develop actions aimed at reducing the impact or severity of the potential problem, we are assuming that there is a potential likelihood that the problem will not be prevented. Because of this possibility, we must search for ways to lessen or minimize the effects of the failure that we couldn't avert. Not all potential problems will be avoidable, so our plan must include provisions to counter the effects.

Consider the example introduced earlier of the single-source supplier of parts or materials. One action might be to develop a secondary supplier to fill the void in the event that the primary supplier isn't able to supply parts and materials. Another consideration might be a redesign of the part that will perform the same function. Still another part of the plan might be to create a safety stock of the critical parts that would keep your processes running until the supplier corrects the problem. If the probability of occurrence is extremely high, then the plan might include steps to replace the supplier. Whatever the case, this is the time for the team to be imaginative and inventive as the plan is developed.

17.4 IDENTIFY DETECTIVE CONTROLS

As pointed out earlier, the purpose of identifying preventive controls is to provide some assurance that any potential failure modes and their related effects are detected early enough in the process to be able to act on them before a crisis evolves and develops. Controls can be fail-safe devices that provide both maximum detection and protection, manual measurements on the process that could be plotted on a control chart, or even audits of the process under consideration.

When attempting to identify an appropriate control, it is important to consider which type is best for the situation or circumstances. We must certainly consider how deleterious or severe the effect(s) might be, but we should also look at the cost to implement the control to detect the negative effect versus the impact of the effect. If the effect isn't considered very harmful, it makes no sense to spend much time or money developing a comprehensive, technical control. On the other hand, if the impact on the organization is considered extreme, then it would make sense to spend the extra time and money.

The most important consideration here is to assess the apparent control and containment needs, then compare these needs to the effectiveness of the existing controls. If there is a disparity or mismatch, then definitive action must be taken to close the gap.

17.5 ESTIMATE OCCURRENCE, SEVERITY, AND DETECTION, THEN RECALCULATE TOTAL RISK FACTOR

When you have formulated actions aimed at preventing, detecting, and reducing the severity of the potential problem, it is time to reevaluate and recalculate the total risk factor. Estimate the probability that the problem will occur, the severity of it if it does occur, and the probability that you will be able to detect it. Evaluate the planned actions and then recalculate the TRF. If the TRF falls into an acceptable range, as dictated in Table 15.4 (Chapter 15), then the plan is probably sound and sensible. If the TRF doesn't fall into an acceptable range, then more creative actions must be developed.

I have a word of caution as you reevaluate each risk factor. Make certain that you and your team are unbiased and objective as you consider the three areas of risk. If you feel or sense that your team isn't being impartial and unbiased, it is always a good idea to get a sanity check from someone outside the group that is not vested in the outcome of the evaluation.

18

Implement Preventive Measures Plan

There comes a moment when you have to stop revving up the car and shove it into gear.

David Mahoney

18.1 FINALIZE AND IMPLEMENT THE PREVENTIVE MEASURES PLAN

As soon as you feel comfortable with the preventive measures plan that your team has developed and reevaluated it for risk, it is time to execute the plan. You have double-checked the plan for its effectiveness, with respect to predicting the chances that the problem will occur, plus your ability to detect it if it does occur. You have also developed actions that are intended to counteract or neutralize the effects of the potential problem if it were to occur. Now it is time to communicate the plan. It's always good practice to hold meetings with key personnel closest to the potential problem to review the purpose and specific actions of the plan before it is actually implemented. If you want the plan to be executed flawlessly, then take the time to make sure that everyone involved clearly understands their roles, tasks, and responsibilities.

After you are convinced that everyone understands the planned actions, my advice is to simply implement your plan and "live in" the process until you are confident that your plan is working effectively. When I say, "live in" the process, I simply mean that you should personally manage the details and minutiae of the plan. My experiences have demonstrated the importance of this action over and over. I have witnessed on numerous occasions good plans gone amiss simply because of how the plan was communicated, so please take the time to methodically and meticulously communicate your plan and then be there during the implementation.

If your control is a measurement or audit, again, be certain that all who perform the control testing first know how to accurately make the measurement, and then measure or audit often in the early stages of implementation. As mentioned earlier, *an ounce of prevention is worth a pound of cure!*

18.2 AUDIT EFFECTIVENESS OF PREVENTION PLAN

Soon after you have executed the preventive measures plan in its entirety, you should know whether or not the plan has been effective and produced the kind of results you had expected and anticipated. But what about the longer-term effectiveness? How can you guarantee that the new methods will continue as planned? There are no guarantees, of course, but it is always a good idea to follow up with periodic audits of the key ingredients and components of the plan, both to be certain that it was implemented in the manner you had planned and that the implementation continues long after the fact.

It is my recommendation that you first make sure that the detection methods are being performed appropriately so that the feedback you are receiving is accurate and reliable. Without high-quality feedback, your reaction to erroneous information may stimulate unwarranted actions. Now is the time to be totally anal and overly cautious of everything in the plan. Being observant, alert, and watchful during and after the implementation will help ensure the plan's success.

19

The Case of the Engineering Backlog

The surest sign of a crisis is that when you have a major problem, no one tries to tell you how to do your job.

Anonymous

19.1 ASKING THE RIGHT QUESTIONS

Solving problems is not always easy work, but it doesn't have to be difficult either. The tools I presented in Chapter 4 will always make life much easier. In this chapter, I will present a case study that is intended to demonstrate the power of asking the right questions, and then by using simple tools, how you can get to the root cause of the problem. Not all problems are quite this easy to solve, but the reality is many of them are; we just make them difficult.

The two tools we are going to use are the run chart and the Pareto chart. In case you don't remember, a run chart is simply a graphical representation of whatever you are measuring, plotted as a function of time. If we were studying product weights, for example, then the run chart would have the actual weight data along the y-axis (vertical) and the corresponding time function (i.e., hours, days, etc.) along the x-axis (horizontal). The Pareto chart visually demonstrates the priority order of a list of items in terms of frequency. (As a side note, I presented a portion of this problem in Chapter 4 to explain the use of run charts. In this chapter, I will present a much more detailed version of the problem.)

19.2 BACKGROUND INFORMATION

This case study involves a company that has been producing truck bodies for the transportation industry since 1958. The truck bodies are designed according to customer-supplied specifications (usually), and then fabricated and installed on bare chassis purchased from various chassis manufacturers. The engineering group is centrally located at the corporate office, and the completed designs are forwarded to the plants electronically. The company produced three basic body types to support the various needs within this industry. The three body types are the stake bodies, which are normally used in applications like landscaping businesses; dry freight bodies, used to haul such things as furniture; and refrigerated bodies used by such businesses as meat companies and fruit haulers.

The company employed seventeen full time engineers (degreed and nondegreed), and the performance metric used to track engineering performance was the amount of backlog hours in an engineering queue. Because the engineering group was in an apparent state of chaos, which I will describe shortly, I was asked to lead this group, but more specifically to reduce the backlog of hours that had grown to an unmanageable level. At the time this problem surfaced, I was the vice president of quality and continuous improvement.

The order process is such that orders are received into the customer service department, evaluated for completeness, and then a decision is made as to whether they are standard truck bodies. If they are standard designs, then no engineering work is required and the order is simply entered into the order entry system, and the truck body is constructed on a truck chassis at one of the seven plants around the country, depending upon which is closer to the point of delivery. Prior to the problem emerging, the normal cycle time to receive the order, build the trucks, and ship them to the customer was approximately three weeks, depending upon the size of the order. If the order required engineering work, then it was forwarded to engineering and placed into a queue, and then remained there until an engineer was available to work on the order. Rather than using a first in, first out (FIFO) process, it was not uncommon for an engineer to go into the order backlog and personally select an order to complete. As you will see, this selection process exacerbated the problem that had developed, because many times the order selected was done so because it was easier for the engineer to complete. As a result, the more difficult orders sat in the queue longer than the simple ones until a customer started screaming for it.

The problem that had developed was that the actual engineering "backlog," as of May 2000, stood at approximately 1200 hours and was growing. To put this number into perspective, since the typical order requiring engineering work averaged approximately three hours to complete, then you will understand the magnitude of this problem. At this rate, there were somewhere around 400 separate orders in the engineering queue waiting to be processed through the engineering department, and most orders were for multiple truck bodies. This backlog translated into lead times to just complete the engineering design work was in excess of forty days or eight weeks. Add another three to four weeks for construction and shipment, and you're looking at a total average cycle time of eleven to twelve weeks to receive, design, and build the truck bodies. This was assuming there were no mistakes in the engineering work, which apparently happened quite frequently. If you were a salesman trying to sell truck bodies, this amount of time would be an inconceivable barrier. Because of this extended lead time, delivery dates were being missed, and the company was rapidly losing market share to its competition. Revenues were obviously declining rapidly as well.

One other concern that I inherited was the declining morale within the engineering group due primarily to excessive overtime the engineers were putting in, which was the root cause of many of the mistakes that were being made on the orders. Of course, when a mistake was made, the order had to go back into this same queue, thus further lengthening the lead time. Many of the engineers had apparently lost their motivation and sense of self-worth. Needless to say, it was a complete mess in engineering.

As I mentioned, during the last week of May 2000, I was asked to assume responsibility for this engineering group. A decision had been made to replace the incumbent vice president of engineering, because of his inability to lead his troops out of this crisis. In other words, the VP had not reduced the backlog that he had inherited from the previous VP, and clearly his group's performance was negatively impacting the financial well-being of the company. I was given the singular mission of reducing the backlog to a manageable level, with manageable being defined as somewhere between 200 and 300 hours. My mandate was clear, but it was also clear that we didn't have much time to accomplish it.

19.3 THE HISTORY AND ANALYSIS OF THE PROBLEM

So here's a question for you. If you were given this problem to solve, how might you go about approaching it, and what might be some of the questions you would ask to get started? Two of the most important questions you might ask both involve the timing of the problem. First, what is the history of this problem? And second, has this problem always been a problem? Then ask yourself, how can I find out the history of this problem, or at least how can I determine how long its actually been a problem?

Whenever you are trying to answer these types of questions, questions that involve time, it is always best if you are able to find existing data from the time period in question, and then construct a run chart to visualize the data. Now, why is this true? Remember Kepner and Tregoe's [1] model for problems? There is a performance level that exists, and then a change occurs, and a new level of performance is observed. The difference between the original performance and the new performance is a deviation. If the deviation is negative, then we declare a problem. A run chart will help you determine if the problem was the result of a change. If no data exists, then you may have to resort to interviews with experienced people. Unfortunately, interview responses are sometimes based upon emotion and opinions, so this is not always fruitful.

Fortunately, for me, this company had years' worth of good data available. The engineering queue data was available by individual months for each calendar year, so I started by combining the past two years worth of data as seen in Figure 19.1. In this run chart of the data from February 1999 through April 2000, there are three numbers plotted as follows:

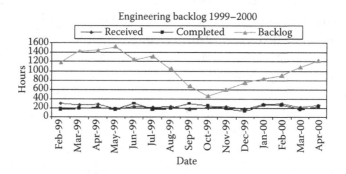

FIGURE 19.1
Engineering backlog February 1999 to April 2000.

1. Hours of orders received
2. Hours of orders completed
3. Hours of backlog in the queue

As can be seen in Figure 19.1, the backlog hours had decreased steadily during the time period from June 1999 through October 1999, but then had progressively increased from that point on, with no signs of slowing down. So, the questions you might ask are, why did the backlog hours decrease?, and why did the backlog hours increase again? Again, the best source for answers to these type questions is always documented evidence, like reports or other written documentation, but in the absence of documentation, we again turn to interviews with experienced employees (i.e., engineers in this case).

In this case, no documentation was available, so we were forced to interview all of the experienced engineers from this time period, and fortunately it did prove to be productive. According to the engineers, the reason for the backlog decrease beginning in June 1999 was an excessive amount of overtime mandated to all engineers (i.e., twenty hours per week per engineer). Although they were able to steer the backlog down, when the decision was made to terminate all overtime (engineers were paid for overtime at this company, so it was costly), not only did the backlog increase to an unacceptable level again, but the morale in engineering became a problem, because they were once again facing pressures and uncertainty. At this point, I decided to look at more history to determine if the problem had always been a problem.

I added three additional years worth of data to the run chart, so it now contained data from January 1996 through May 2000. Based upon what you see in this expanded run chart (Figure 19.2), what conclusions are

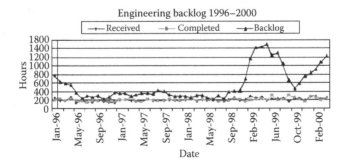

FIGURE 19.2
Engineering backlog January 1996 to February 2000.

you able to draw? Between June 1996 and December 1998, does the engineering backlog appear to be under control and "manageable"? And what about the question about whether the problem has always been a problem? I'm sure you'll agree with me that the problem has not always been a problem. As you will see, this realization was an extraordinarily important discovery.

If one were to ask, when did the problem start?, then we see that the problem began in earnest in January 1999. So, by simply plotting the data on a run chart, we are able to pinpoint the time frame of when the engineering hours backlog actually became a problem (remember that problems of this nature begin with a change).

Ask yourself this question: If I want to solve this problem, then what must my next question be? If you said, what changed on or around January 1999? then you answered the question correctly. So, how do we or can we find out what changed in January 1999? Finding engineering documentation would be the best way, but unfortunately many companies don't keep good records, and this company was no exception. So sometimes, once again, we must rely on interviews with employees who were present when the change occurred, and that is exactly what we did.

The time period between May 1996 and December 1998, when we did not have the problem, is considered a defect-free configuration (DFC). You will recall that a DFC is, in this case, found by asking the question, when would you expect to see the problem, but you don't? The presence of a DFC begs the question, what is unique or distinct when comparing when the problem exists to when it doesn't exist? Based upon the presence of this apparent DFC, our next course of action was to determine what were the *distinctions* or differences that existed between the two periods of time.

There was little, if any, documentation available that could lead us to understand what had changed or what the distinctions were, so we, again, conducted one-on-one interviews with engineers and other support groups that were present when this change apparently had transpired. The interviews revealed the following:

1. Prior to January 1999, all incoming orders were received and processed by a single group within engineering. The new engineering VP, wanting to make some changes (and make a name for himself), "restructured" engineering by creating three individual groups to handle incoming orders:
   Group 1: Stake body orders only

Group 2: Refrigerated body orders only

Group 3: Dry freight body orders only

2. The engineering manager staffed all three groups equally (i.e., same number of engineers in each group).

3. The engineering VP failed to consider that the incoming orders were not of equal complexity or numbers for all three body types.

Because there were now three separate groups that had become "specialists," three distinct silos had been created within engineering, with no provision or arrangement for intragroup communication. The result of this "silo" creation was the development of a significant backlog for dry freight bodies. This comprised the bulk of the backlog hours.

Figure 19.3 is a Pareto chart of the distribution of orders for each group. It really doesn't take a rocket scientist to see that if the groups are staffed equally and the numbers of incoming orders is over 60% straight (or dry freight) bodies, then a backlog or bottleneck will occur within these type bodies. It's exactly the same result one would expect from a constraint operation in a manufacturing process.

So, faced with this problem and not much time available to fix it, what would your solution be? Would you try and relive the past? Sort of, "If it ain't broke, don't fix it!" We did just that! We simply went back in time and recreated the system that worked so well before. We did several things immediately:

1. We immediately returned to the single group concept and beefed up the group from six to seventeen engineers and focused everyone on the backlog orders (i.e., no new hires).

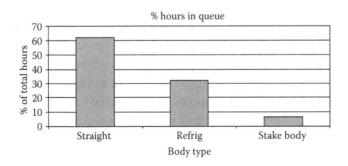

FIGURE 19.3

Pareto chart of percent hours in queue by body type.

2. We developed a daily target graph so that each engineer could measure and see the group's daily performance progress.
3. We determined that there were thirteen late appraisals in engineering (two were at least six months late), and mandated completion of all of them within two days (remember I said morale was very low?).

So, let's summarize what has happened thus far in our search for the root cause of this problem.

1. Our first step was to define the problem to be the engineering hour's backlog was excessive. As a matter of fact, we defined the current state to be in excess of 1200 hours, and that in order for this problem to be considered resolved, it had to be at a manageable level of between 200 and 300 hours. We also had identified a secondary problem of low engineering morale.
2. The second thing we did was to begin collecting facts from existing data and documentation in the form of a run chart so we could see some history. The run chart clearly demonstrated when the problem began. This was important to us, because once we defined when the problem began, we could begin to look for changes that had occurred that could have produced the effect (i.e., excessive engineering queue hours). We said that if we could determine what had changed, then we could probably reverse the changes and correct the problem.
3. We then determined the changes that had taken place by conducting interviews of engineers and support groups that were in place when the engineering hours began to become excessive. We would have liked to have confirmed this with documentation, but in its absence, conversations and recollections proved to be helpful. We determined that a significant change in the organizational structure of the engineering group had occurred just prior to the onset of the problem. We asked ourselves the question, "Could the change that occurred have created the effect we are seeing?" and the answer was yes it could have. The next step was to change the organization back to its original structure and to begin measuring the response to the change (i.e., one single group within engineering to handle all incoming orders and a run chart with a daily target line, so that engineers could see their progress).

The next step was to measure the progress or response to this change. Figure 19.4 is a run chart that includes a total hour's target line, total hours

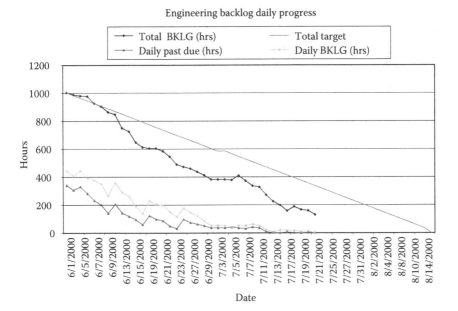

FIGURE 19.4
Engineering backlog by day.

backlog, daily past due, and a daily hour's backlog. As you can see, the results were pretty astounding. The results came immediately, as the backlog decreased from 1200 hours to less than 200 hours in eleven weeks and remained within the acceptable limits. Figure 19.5 is an extended plot of hours through the end of September 2000, and it is clear that stability was regained and engineering hours were, once again, manageable. The most significant result, however, was in the reduction in lead times for order processing that was reduced from forty days to an astonishing forty-eight hours. What was once a problem for the company was now a differentiator in the marketplace that stimulated sales rather than being a barrier. All of this from a run chart, a Pareto chart, and a few simple questions.

One final point regarding the success of this engineering problem-solving experience. Figure 19.6 is a plot of hours received, hours completed, and backlog hours. One thing that stands out as being totally significant is this. Remember, I had mentioned that this success had actually stimulated sales? If you look at Figure 19.6 closely, you will notice that at no time prior to the resolution of this problem were the number of hours received and completed anywhere near the volumes observed after the problem was corrected. As a matter of fact, the average hours received

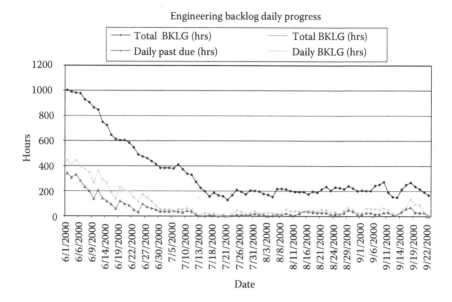

FIGURE 19.5
Engineering backlog by day.

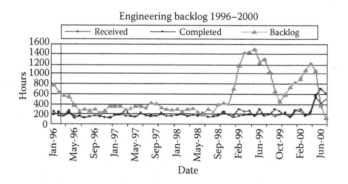

FIGURE 19.6
Engineering backlog by month.

and processed out of engineering averaged just over 300 hours when the engineering process was stable (i.e., between June 1996 and December 1998), but when the problem was corrected and sales were stimulated, at one point this number reached approximately 800 hours. These additional hours were not only managed, but the group was able to absorb and complete them, with no overtime and no engineers added. Not only was the process "fixed," it was improved. The improvement methodology that was utilized is another subject completely, as tools like value analysis and value stream mapping were used to significantly reduce the amount of non-value-added work within engineering.

To summarize then, this case study was an exercise in problem analysis by following a systematic and structured approach. The key steps included:

1. Problem definition
2. Problem description
3. Determination of changes relative to when the problem started (run chart)
4. Discovery of defect-free configurations and the distinctions between when we had the problem compared to when we didn't (run chart and Pareto chart)
5. Collection of key information to generate possible causes (interviews, causal chain)
6. Testing for most probable cause
7. Verification of the true root cause
8. Implementing the solution (reversing the change that created the problem)
9. Implementing a control (run chart with target line and daily feedback)

This simple, straightforward process enabled this company to not only determine the root cause of its problem, but it also facilitated improvement that ultimately resulted in a much improved process. Instead of treating the symptoms of the problem (i.e., overtime to reduce the deteriorating engineering queue hours) as the original leadership had done, the new leadership attacked the problem head-on with this systematic approach, and the problem was solved.

Notice that in this case study I didn't use all of the steps in the Problem Solving Roadmap, simply because they weren't all needed. Whenever the sense of urgency is high, as it was in this case, it is perfectly acceptable to use the steps in the roadmap that get the job done. Because the engineering hours in the run chart had spiked up, I knew that the problem was the result of a change, so the only real course of action was to find that change and reverse it, and it worked.

Problem analysis facilitates the task of gathering and evaluating information about problems, but if we are unable to track down the key facts needed to solve a problem, then the problem will persist and defy resolution. No approach or process, however applied, will solve a problem, unless a systematic and structured approach to problem solving is followed.

And if you do follow this systematic approach to problem solving, your chances of actually solving the problem are greatly enhanced.

One last comment, or question I should say. As a result of the changes to the internal structure of the engineering group, what do you think happened to the morale of the group? The answer is that it improved dramatically. All performance appraisals were brought up to date, but the real reason for the morale improvement was that the engineers were, once again, feeling good about themselves, because they were producing good results.

20

The Case of the Defective Pinions

It is better to solve problems than crises.

John Guinther

20.1 CASE BACKGROUND

Improvement, in any endeavor, requires a detailed knowledge of the current situation and a team that understands the intricacies of the process. That is to say, if improvement is to occur, then adequate data on problems that exist must be collected so that problems can be defined and the correct priority established. This data must include things like information on where and what the problems are, the severity and frequency of the problems, and the impact of the problems if resolution is achieved. This case involved a subsupplier of pinions to a major European auto manufacturer. Pinions are used in things like turn signals and headlight levers. The pinions, in question, had five individual diameters along the surface of the shaft that were repeatedly wandering outside the customer specification limits and had to be either reworked or scrapped. The company's major customer was not pleased with the quality of the pinions and on-time delivery rate, and was threatening to source another supplier. My job was to help the auto company understand the nature of this problem, and develop and implement an immediate and lasting solution. As usual, with problems of this nature there was an intense sense of urgency.

When I arrived at the facility in France, the only data collection in place was limited to general information regarding scrap and downtime. The scrap and downtime being collected included the total amount by shift and date, but not any specific information as to why it had occurred.

The only exception to this was the existence of finished product inspection data, which included both the amount of scrap and the general reason it was scrapped. For example, the scrap data might state that it was scrapped for diameter, but not which diameter. There was nothing in place to demonstrate the specific causes for scrap or downtime at each of the individual process steps. Without this type of specific information, it would be nearly impossible to define, prioritize, and ultimately resolve the problems with scrap and downtime.

20.2 ESTABLISHMENT OF A DATA COLLECTION SYSTEM

Our first action, then, was to develop and implement a simple process for collecting rework, scrap, and downtime information by cause code. I developed a simple data collection system that listed the cause and amount of downtime, rework, and scrap. Implementing this data collection process was far from simple and much more difficult than I had anticipated, because there were numerous false starts in this process. That is, when asked if the system had been explained in detail to all operators, I was told that it had been. It didn't take long to determine that not all operators, supervisors, and maintenance mechanics had been informed, so much of the preliminary information was incomplete. In fairness, part of the problem was a language issue, being that I am not especially fluent in French. But at the end of the day, the system was implemented to my satisfaction.

Even after the system was implemented, when new operators were working on the machines, the communications to them about the new procedure was inconsistent or nonexistent. I mention this just to reinforce the importance of leadership involvement and effective communication in any problem-solving event. I finally had to involve the chief operating officer of the company, who mandated that the data collection be done correctly, and we collected the data.

After the data collection system was finally in place, and one week's worth of data was collected, it was apparent that the process step requiring the most attention was grinding (rectification) on two supposedly identical grinding machines. Not only did this process step account for the most in-process scrap, but the levels of downtime were so excessive at times that this facility was forced to utilize outside subcontractors in order to produce and ship enough pinions to their customers. At one point, up to

1000 parts per day were being sent outside the facility to an independent subcontractor for grinding. This turned out to be a very expensive undertaking, so timely resolution of this problem was critical.

20.3 SCRAP SUMMARY AND ANALYSIS

The purpose of the grinding machine is to grind the pinions to each of their final five diameters. Historically, the number one source of rework, scrap, and downtime had been because the diameters, measured in five locations along the surface of the pinions, had been either too small or too large. Data collection, by specific cause, was initiated on the two supposedly identical grinders, and it was determined that the scrap rates for the diameters on each machine were considerably different. Grinder number 1 averaged 5.1%, while grinder number 2 averaged 3.1%.

According to the quality manager of this facility, the problem of inconsistent diameters had been a problem on both grinders since the day they were installed, but because data wasn't analyzed routinely, he was surprised by the different scrap rates between the two grinders. Because no specific data existed to support this notion, it was necessary to collect specific scrap and rework information before actions could be taken. There were five distinctly different diameters, and each contributed to the overall scrap, rework, and downtime on these two machines. In addition to the scrap and rework costs, the company was continually required to air freight shipments of pinions to avoid late charges and line shutdowns at their customer's facility, so the cost of this problem was extremely high.

One of the first priorities was to establish which of the five different diameters (if not all) were causing the problems. Table 20.1 summarizes each of the diameters and tolerance limits. Based upon the tolerance bandwidths,

TABLE 20.1

Diameter Tolerances

Diameter	Lower Limit of Tolerance	Upper Limit of Tolerance
1	−0.005	+0.000
2	−0.000	+0.010
3	−0.005	+0.000
4	+0.002	+0.011
5	−0.008	+0.000

I surmised that the two diameters that probably had accounted for the majority of scrap would most likely be the two locations (diameters 1 and 3) with the diameter tolerance band width of only 0.005 mm (5 microns). The data collection revealed this assumption to in fact be true.

Figure 20.1 is a summary of scrap information by cause on grinder 2. (Note: I have left the causes of scrap in French to add an element of realism.) As you can see in Figure 20.1, the number one cause of scrap on grinder 2 between October 7 and 11, 2003, was ø *Non-Retouche*, which in French translated to diameters that were not repairable, because the diameters were too small. The second leading cause of scrap, ø *Retouch* means that the pinion was repairable, but the repair had failed. Again, this scrap was a diameter problem, as was the third cause, *Reglage* (adjustment). Of the 252 scraps that occurred during this time period, 242 (96%) were caused by the grinder's failure to meet diameters 1 and 3, just as I had predicted.

With this information in hand, it was clear that we needed to look at the capability of this machine to hold the 5-micron tolerance. During the same time frame, grinder 1 was not producing parts because of another technical problem, so we focused on grinder 2, assumed that the same problems existed on grinder 1, and concluded that we could translate our findings from grinder 2 to grinder 1.

The most recent process capability that had been run on the grinders had been performed three months prior to my arrival and the results indicated a total lack of process capability. The purpose of the capability study is simply to ascertain how well a process will produce parts that conform to specification. Two of the calculations frequently used are the Pp and Ppk. In simplistic terms, the Pp tells us how well the process could produce parts if it were perfectly centered, while the Ppk is a measure of how

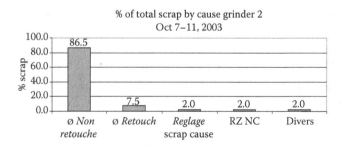

FIGURE 20.1
Pareto chart of percent of scrap by cause for grinder 2.

well the process is actually performing. A value of 1.0 for either of the two indices suggests that the ends of the normal distribution of data from the process will coincide exactly with the limits of the tolerance band. So, any value less than 1.0 indicates that the process will produce some parts that are unacceptable, and a value greater than 1.0 signifies that all measurements on the parts will fall within the upper and lower limits of the specification. If the values for Pp and Ppk are significantly below 1.0, then it is safe to say that many parts will be defective.

The minimum target for both of these capability indices is 1.33, so that if the process shifts naturally or if adjustments are purposely made to center the process, then the process will continue to produce acceptable parts. It is also assumed that the process is free of special cause variation and, therefore, contains only natural variation.

Table 20.2 summarizes the capability indices for all five of the diameters measured on the two grinders. Because the capability indices on grinder 2 are significantly better than grinder 1, we would expect to experience more diameter scraps on grinder 1 compared to grinder 2, and that was precisely the case. Remember that the scrap levels on grinder 1 were approximately five percent compared to three percent on grinder 2. However, based upon the Pp and Ppk values on grinder 1, one might also expect to see diameter scraps in locations other than the ø 21.02. Since this was not occurring, I questioned the validity of the capability studies or that improvements had been made since the study was run. It was my opinion that the capability

TABLE 20.2

Diameter Tolerances versus Pp and Ppk

Diameter	Tolerance + Limits	Pp	Ppk
Grinder 2			
1	ø22.00 + 0.002 + 0.011	1.19	1.11
2	ø12.00 + 0.000 + 0.008	1.08	1.05
3	ø21.02 + 0.000 − 0.005	0.71	0.49
4	ø22.315 + 0.005 − 0.005	1.65	0.70
5	ø21.02 + 0.000 − 0.005	0.70	0.56
Grinder 1			
1	ø22.00 + 0.002 + 0.011	0.71	0.72
2	ø12.00 + 0.000 + 0.008	0.67	0.63
3	ø21.02 + 0.000 − 0.005	0.53	0.48
4	ø22.315 + 0.005 − 0.005	0.88	0.39
5	ø21.02 + 0.000 − 0.005	0.57	0.42

values were closer to 1.0, in the case of diameters 3 and 5, and probably greater than 1.0 on the other diameters.

When capability indices are close to 1.0, it is not uncommon to see more scraps caused by overadjusting the process, especially if the decision to adjust the process is based upon single data points. I surmised that in the normal operation of the grinders, if the grinder operator had a single scrap for the diameter being too large, then an adjustment was probably made to reduce the diameter. When the adjustment was made, the population of the data shifted to a smaller diameter, which caused scrap diameters in the opposite direction (i.e., too small). I observed several operators on grinder 2 and found this to be the case. Each time a scrap would occur in either direction, an adjustment was made in the opposite direction to the grinder for the diameter 21.02 and predictably more scraps were created.

One way to improve this situation was to base all adjustment decisions on sample averages, rather than single point measurements since the sample average is an estimate of the population average. Between October 11 and October 16, a study was run instructing the operators to not make adjustments when they had a single scrap but rather to let the grinders run normally, collect data on the next four pinions, and then calculate the sample average. If the average of the five measurements was outside the specification limits, then the operators were to make their normal adjustment. (Note: Since each individual pinion was automatically measured, I knew that the grinder would alert the operator to each out-of-tolerance pinion diameter, so there was no worry about defective material reaching the customer.) Prior to the study, we reset the grinder to produce diameters as close to the center of the specification as possible. The rationale behind this move was that if we wanted to simulate the best possible running condition, then centering the process would produce the greatest number of good parts.

Figure 20.2 is the run chart of this data that depicts the percent scrap before, during, and after this study. Prior to running this study, for the previous 8243 pinions there were a total of 242 scraps for diameter or 2.94% of production. During the study, for the 10,524 pinions produced, there were a total of 86 scraps or 0.82% of production. Immediately after the study, on the 8683 pinions produced there were a total of 373 scraps for diameter or 4.3% of production.

Based upon the results of this study, it was apparent that the company, without spending any money, could improve its scrap levels and outgoing quality simply by applying some very basic laws of process control and,

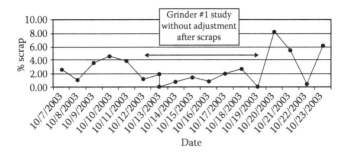

FIGURE 20.2
Percent of production scrapped for diameter on grinder 1.

more specifically, changing the rules of action for when and when not to make machine adjustments. This did not preclude the need to improve the capability of the grinders, but for now an immediate benefit could be realized by simply changing the rules of action.

Clearly this study had demonstrated how overadjustment of a process will actually cause the process to deteriorate and produce defective parts. If the process Cpk (or Ppk) were equal to 1.0, and the process mean was identical to the center of the specification. For example, the laws of the normal distribution tell us that it would be normal to produce 3 pinions out of 1000 (0.003%) that would fall outside the tolerance limits. Since this process is producing parts outside the tolerance at a rate of approximately 0.8%, we would estimate the Cpk to be somewhere between 0.8 and 0.9 with the process relatively centered. For example, if the process average was 21.0174 and the standard deviation was 0.0009, then the short-term Cpk would be 0.85 and the percentage of parts being produced outside the limits for this diameter would be approximately 0.79%.

The real problem on these two grinders was the excessive amount of variation within the process with respect to the tolerance width, and in this case, most of the excessive variation was being caused by an operator or supervisor overadjusting the process. One of the basic laws of probability and/or SPC is to never adjust the process on the basis of single point measurements but rather on an average of several parts. If the calculated sample average is unacceptable, then the process should clearly be adjusted. Conversely, if the sample average is acceptable, then the process should be permitted to run without adjustment.

On the basis of this analysis, it was apparent that a problem-solving team needed to be formed to attack this problem head on. A team was formed that consisted of the grinder 2 operator, the supervisor from the area, the quality manager, the plant manager, an engineer, and me. The results of this study and current situation were presented to the team, and then a root cause analysis was completed. The problem analysis flowchart (PAF) (Figure 20.3) was the tool used by the problem-solving team that I had developed and translated into French. (Note: For details on how to use a PAF chart, reference Chapter 6 in my first book, *Process Problem Solving: A Guide for Maintenance and Operations Teams* [2].)

The first step in any meaningful problem-solving event is the development of the problem statement. In this case, after hearing a description of the problem, the team concluded that the problem was excessive variation in the diameter of the pinions run on grinders 1 and 2. To this end, the team filled out the remaining steps of the PAF chart (see Figure 20.3).

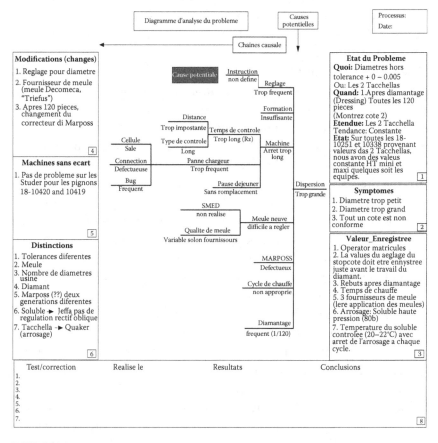

FIGURE 20.3
Problem analysis flowchart.

As with the Pareto chart presented earlier, for realism the PAF chart is presented in French, just as the team developed it. The specifics of what actually occurred in this case study aren't nearly as important as the process of following a structured approach to problem solving. The customary questions of what, where, and when, and scope of the problem were answered, and a problem statement was developed. The team investigated and listed symptoms of the problem and any relevant data it believed was important. The team also listed any known changes that could have impacted the grinders or problem with diameters. Next, the team identified two defect-free configurations (two other type pinions with more forgiving diameter tolerances) and the distinctions between where the problem existed and where it didn't.

The team was now ready to create a causal chain. The causal chain portrays the potential failure modes and concerns of the team members, as explained in Chapter 4, and then answers the question why until arriving at a potential root cause. For example, the operator and supervisor, after seeing the scrap data and basic SPC theory I had presented, believed that the operators were making diameter adjustments too frequently. When the question why was asked, it was clear that operator instructions on when to make the adjustments were not defined. That was an action that could be acted upon and is a potential root cause of the problem.

Continuing down the causal chain, other potential root causes were defined and corrective actions were developed. For example, since the pinions were made of steel, there was a concern that if the machine is permitted to be down for extended periods of time, then the diameters on the parts could be affected by temperature changes. One of the reasons for the grinders being down was that the operators must shut down the grinder three times every two hours and measure the surface state of the pinions in the lab. In order to do this, the operator had to leave his or her machine, take a sample to the test lab, and then measure the surface profile themselves. This takes approximately three minutes for the grinder operator to accomplish, but could easily have been completed by quality control workers. This procedure was changed, thus eliminating the need for the machine to be shut down. In addition to the potential quality improvement, there was also a gain in production of nine pieces every two hours, since the machine can now continue to run instead of being shut down during the measurement. Over the course of a full production day, the increase in pinion production would be over 100 pinions on each grinder, or over 200 additional pinions per day without adding additional labor.

Another potential cause for excessive variation was the device used to automatically measure diameters during the grinding cycle (i.e., a poka yoke–type device). The device had been mounted on the ø 12 section of the pinion instead of on the diameters producing the most scrap. The tolerance for this diameter had a range of 0.008 mm compared to 0.005 on the problem diameters. Because of this, it was suggested that the team meet with the supplier of the measurement device to determine if the measurement could be made on one of the 21.02 mm diameters.

Although the grinder problem-solving team was still in its early stages of implementing the recommended actions, significant improvements had already been observed. Figure 20.4 is a run chart of percent scrap due to diameters from October 26 until November 1, 2003. The new scrap reaction technique employed on both grinders is depicted on the chart, and since implementing this new technique, the daily average percent scrap for diameter problems had decreased from 3.1% to 0.73% and appears to be stable at this level.

Grinder 1 displayed an even greater percentage improvement as is depicted in Figure 20.5. The reduction on grinder 1 was much more

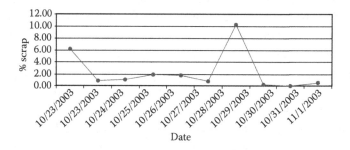

FIGURE 20.4
Grinder 2 diameter scrap by day.

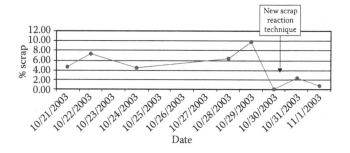

FIGURE 20.5
Grinder 1 percent of scrap for diameter.

dramatic than grinder 2, because the initial scrap levels were much higher. The average scrap levels on this grinder had been reduced from nearly 6% to less than 1% and appear to have stabilized as well. The level of scrap on grinder 1 since implementing the new scrap reaction technique is even better than Figure 20.5 represents. On October 31, the day shift shop manager, in an effort to improve throughput, changed the cycle time, and immediately twenty scraps resulted. Without this change, the percent of scrap on grinders 1 and 2 would have been nearly identical.

As of October 31, 2003, the level of scrap for diameters had been reduced on grinder 1 from 3.1 percent to 0.73 percent and on grinder 2 from 5.1 percent to 0.82 percent with zero euros spent. In terms of numbers of pinions per day saved with these actions, the combined total number of acceptable pieces had increased, on average, by over 500 pinions per day!

At the same time the scrap and rework problem existed, another problem on these same two grinders was unplanned downtime that had been out-of-control for some time. In addition to the scrap information data, collection for downtime by cause was also implemented on these two machines. We were able to demonstrate that over seventy percent of the downtime had been caused by the same diameter problems. Over a period of three weeks, grinder 2 had experienced downtime for diameter problems, totaling approximately 29 hours while on grinder 1 the total was approximately 22 hours. Since the average cycle times on grinders 2 and 1 were 33 and 30 seconds respectively, unplanned downtime for this cause alone had resulted in the loss of approximately 3163 pinions on grinder 2 in 20 days (158/day) and 2640 pinions on grinder 1 in 26 days (103/day).

If the downtime for diameter adjustments on these two grinders had only been reduced by seventy percent, then the potential increase in daily output is approximately 183 pinions per day. Therefore, by improving the two grinders' ability to produce pinions within the specifications, the total potential throughput increase from scrap and downtime reduction was approximately 260 pinions per day, or nearly 1600 pinions per week, and this team had other improvement actions yet to be implemented. If anyone ever has reservations about whether a correlation between quality and production throughput exists, this should dispel the doubt.

I followed up on this supplier several months later and learned that the team had continued their improvement efforts and the results continued to demonstrate improved quality and reduced unplanned downtime. They had met with the supplier of the measurement device and were able to move it to the smaller diameter on the pinion and achieved even more positive results in both quality and unplanned downtime. As a matter of fact, as a result of this team's actions, the total throughput increase had ballooned to almost 3000 additional pinions per week. Remember the irate customer, the one that had threatened to move its business to another supplier? Because of the improved outgoing quality and decreased unplanned downtime, on-time shipments had increased dramatically without the need for premium freight. But the good news here was that orders from this customer had also increased significantly. Once again, by following a structured and systematic approach to problem solving, remarkable results were achieved by very ordinary people.

21

The Case of the Cracking Rails

The most complicated problems will arise at the most remote locations.

Joe Cooch

21.1 INTRODUCTION TO CASE STUDY

In this chapter, we will look at a very interesting case study concerning a company that had actually solved a problem, but because the company didn't understand how to perform a structured root cause analysis or analyze existing data, it had no idea the problem had been corrected. In fact, the company continued to make process and design changes that only complicated the situation. This is a case study about a company that makes stainless steel, mild steel, and aluminum over-the-road tanker truck wagons for both the petroleum (gasoline, etc.) and food industries (juices, milks, etc.). The company designs, fabricates, and assembles the tankers at two separate facilities that, for anonymity purposes, we will designate as plant A and plant B.

When I arrived at the company's main facility (plant B), a team had already been formed whose primary objective was to study, understand, and solve a warranty problem that had existed at both of its two manufacturing facilities for quite some time. This particular team had been formed because of the latest in a line of the many complaints and warranty claims for this problem that they had just received. The problem, as defined by the team, was *premature cracking and failure of a mounting rail*. The singular purpose of the mounting rail is the primary means of mounting the tank to the frame.

In addition to solving this problem, the company had also wanted me to teach the team how to follow a structured and systematic approach to solving problems. As you will see, the team was able to successfully identify several root causes and identify the solution that it had accidentally implemented several years ago by following a systematic and structured approach as outlined in Figure 21.1.

The Problem Solving Roadmap consists of six major sections and seventeen individual steps. Completion of each major section will yield different milestones or deliverables as the individual steps are completed. In section I, for example, there are two deliverables: the problem statement and a success metric. The problem-solving team continues through the roadmap until the most probable cause is identified and a solution is implemented. In the final section, the roadmap guides the team to develop a control to prevent the recurrence of the problem, thus making the roadmap a closed-loop corrective action tool.

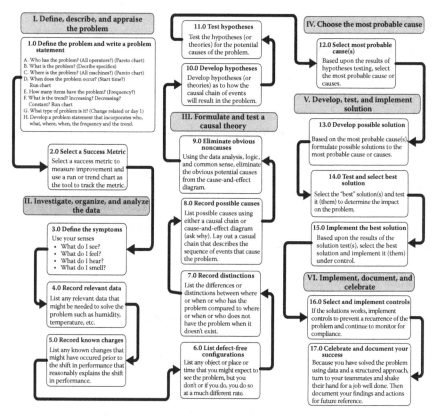

FIGURE 21.1
Problem solving roadmap.

21.2 DEFINE, DESCRIBE, AND APPRAISE THE PROBLEM

The first requirement when attempting to solve any problem is to make certain that everyone agrees on the definition of the problem so that each person's focus and understanding of the problem is exactly the same. The team systematically gathered and reviewed all of the available data, which in this case was warranty records, photos, and so forth, and were able to determine approximately when the problem had started and, to its surprise, ended. Determining *when* the cracking problem began (and, in this case ended) provided valuable information for the team. The team did this by first arranging the warranty claims for cracked rails, in production order, and then plotted them on a run chart.

21.3 INVESTIGATE, ORGANIZE, AND ANALYZE THE DATA

Figures 21.2 and 21.3 are run charts from each plant depicting the mounting rail warranty claims by month and year for plant B and plant A, respectively. Since the dates listed in the run charts are the dates the tanks were manufactured at each location, the team gained valuable insight relative to the current status of the problem. For plant B, there had not been a warranty claim for this problem since November 2001, but one of plant A's customers had rejected a tank for a cracked rail that had been fabricated and assembled in February 2003.

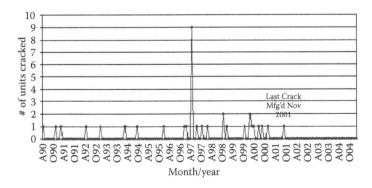

FIGURE 21.2
Plant B angle rail cracking by month/year.

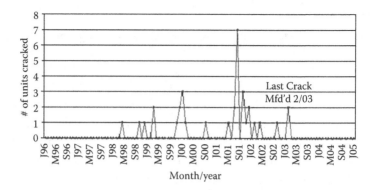

FIGURE 21.3
Plant A mounting angle rail cracks by month/year.

From these two charts, it appeared as though the cracking problem had stopped in plant B, but not yet in plant A. The team continued its investigation and determined that all of the most recent plant A failures had only been detected on mild steel rails and none on stainless steel rails. This was an enormously important discovery, because this information would allow the team to focus its problem-solving efforts on mild steel rails, only in this plant. That is, if the team was going to unravel this problem on the mild steel tankers in plant A, then it needed to uncover what the changes were in plant B to correct the same problem on mild steel tanker wagons. The team would also need to search for and locate the design and process distinctions between plant A and plant B that were related to mild steel rails. As a final point, it would be of the essence that both plants work to collectively determine what change or changes had been made to correct the cracking problem on stainless steel tankers at both locations.

As a point of distinction, remember in Chapter 2 when I described a change-related problem, and I told you that if you are able to determine what had changed that you could certainly determine the root cause? Having said this, remember that the inverse is true as well. That is, if there was a change made that corrected the problem, then you can use the same tools and techniques to determine when and what change had been made. This is in reality just as significant as finding the root cause of a problem. If this team was not able to segregate and pinpoint the change that had "fixed" the problem, then the probability that the problem would return would be almost a certainty. So, remember this as we go forward with this case study.

The next action for the team was to observe all of the available photos, warranty claims, and other pertinent information so that a profile of the

FIGURE 21.4
Cracking example.

problem could be developed (i.e., what the problem was, where it was happening, and when it was happening). In doing so, the team determined that all of the cracks (i.e., the what of the problem) had occurred on the front of the mounting rail along the weld seam (i.e., the where of the problem). Figure 21.4 is a representative photo of the cracking that the team had observed. The most common crack had occurred at the mounting rail weld and continued to propagate along various lengths of the weld. The team now had the information it needed to develop its problem statement as follows:

> Problem statement—Premature cracking and failure of the mounting rail weld, on units made in plant A (since 1998) and plant B (since 1990). No customer complaints have been observed on plant B stainless or mild steel subframes manufactured since November 2001, but the problem is still observed on plant A mild steel tankers.

21.4 SYMPTOMS AND RELEVANT DATA

The team subsequently assembled a list of symptoms and data that might be used to understand and solve this problem. The most significant symptoms of this problem and relevant data were as follows:

1. There were marks around the mounting bolts resembling an overtorque condition.
2. Eighty-six percent of the failures were on air ride suspensions.
3. Eighty-two percent of the failures were on stainless versus mild steel.

21.5 RECORD ALL KNOWN CHANGES

The team then investigated and developed a list of all known changes and modifications to the design of the rail or relevant process steps or components. In doing so, the team was able to theorize why the incidence of cracking, had either stopped or declined. The following change was identified: Plant B and plant A changed from ⅜ inch rails to ¼ inch rails on stainless steel tanks in the fall of 2002. This was the only change that had been made to the design of the tanker wagons in the immediate area of where the cracking had been observed. No changes to the build process were found.

21.6 SEARCH FOR AND RECORD DEFECT-FREE CONFIGURATIONS (DFCs)

You will recall that defect-free configurations (DFCs) are where or when you might expect to see the problem, but you don't. For example, the team had recognized that all known cracks had occurred at the front of the rail, so you might anticipate seeing the same cracks at the rear of the rail. Since there were no cracks at the rear of the rail, then this location would be considered a DFC. The team brainstormed and developed the following list of DFCs:

1. The rear end of the mounting rail
2. Plant B stainless and mild steel rails since November 2001
3. Plant A stainless steel rails since February 2003

The existence of DFCs told the team that there were significant differences or distinctions between where or when you have the problem compared to where or when you don't. By finding the distinctions the team could determine the root cause, so it was imperative that the team determine all of the distinctions that existed.

21.7 SEARCH FOR AND RECORD DISTINCTIONS

The team evaluated the existing materials, fabrication assembly processes, and the mounting rail designs, and exposed the following differences between plant B and plant A for mild steel rails:

1. Plant B employs a ⅜ bend radius, whereas plant A uses a ½ inch bend radius.
2. Plant B uses flex core wire for welding the rails, whereas Plant A uses hard wire.

Although these differences existed between the two plants, the team was now challenged to determine if, in fact, these differences could explain the performance differences between the two facilities on mild steel rails.

21.8 RECORD POSSIBLE ROOT CAUSES

The next step for the team was to develop a list of potential root causes through the use of a causal chain. The team began by listing the problem on the right side of the causal chain and then continued asking why until a potential root cause was determined. As can be seen in the causal chain (Figure 20.4), the team identified six separate chains as follows:

1. Welding point stress too high
2. Design not robust enough
3. Mounting rail angle warped
4. Residual stress present
5. Mounting rail weld undercut
6. Mounting angle rail weight limit exceeded

As mentioned, the team continued the causal chains leftward, continuing to ask why until it arrived at a potential root cause. The team then developed action items or tests that had to be run, as depicted in Figure 21.5.

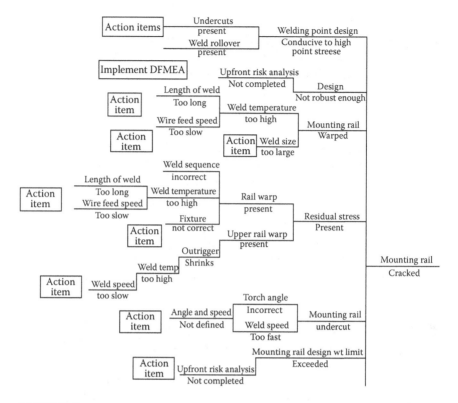

FIGURE 21.5
Causal chain for mounting rail cracking.

21.9 DEVELOP HYPOTHESES FOR ROOT CAUSES

The team reviewed all assignments and data plots, including run charts of cracks by month and year for plant A and plant B, and matrices of configurations and characteristics, and performed numerous stress analyses. The team then developed two lists, using the assumption that *the only rails that have cracked are the ones reported as warranty claims.* Since there was no way of knowing whether other mounting rails had cracked but weren't reported, this was a logical assumption. The two lists were (1) things we know to be true and (2) things we believe to be true. The lists were as follows:

Things We Know to be True

- The last plant B crack was manufactured in November 2001.
- The last plant A crack was manufactured in February 2003.

- The last stainless-steel rail crack was manufactured in August 2002 from either plant.
- Frame rails of 104 inches have never cracked (9 to 10 years).
- Cracks are more probable on air rides (sixty-two of seventy-two were on air rides).
- Cracks are more probable on stainless steel than mild steel (fifty-nine of seventy-two).
- All cracks have been on ³⁄₁₆ inch rails, and none on ¼ inch rails.
- Suspension brand is independent of cracking.
- Plant A uses hardwire and plant B uses core wire.
- Cracks are on the front end only (none on the rear end).
- Plant B and plant A subframe department's welding techniques are the same.
- Plant B's bend radius is ⅜ inch and plant A's is ½ inch.

Things We Believe to be True

- Reinforcing angle plus ¼ inch rails stopped the cracks.
- Cracks are independent of tire size.
- Cracks are independent of axle spreads.
- Heavy gross applications are more probable to have cracks on plant A's units.
- Units manufactured with truck mount design (before 1998) did not crack.

The team was challenged to attempt to understand why what we know and believe to be true are in fact true, and then to develop theories as to why the cracking is occurring. The team brainstormed and concluded the following:

- Because the last cracked rail in plant B was manufactured in November 2001 and in February 2003 in plant A, it was clear that there were distinctions or differences in the design or manufacturing processes or both. The team was able to determine that the most significant difference between the two plants was that the main subframe rail bend radius in plant A was ½ inch and ⅜ inch in plant B. Stress analysis confirmed that there was a significant reduction in stress on the mounting rail weld when moving from the ½ inch radius to the ⅜ inch radius when using a ³⁄₁₆ inch rail. On the basis of this improvement, it is concluded that plant A should convert to the ⅜ inch bend radius.

- The team identified that in 2002, both plant B and plant A, in an effort to eliminate this cracking problem, made two changes. Both facilities moved away from 3/16 to 1/4 inch mounting rails on stainless steel rails only (i.e., not mild steel) and began welding undermount doublers (two on the front and two on the back) to further reduce the stress on the welds. Stress analysis confirmed that both of these changes significantly reduced the applied stresses on the welds and clearly stopped the cracking problem on stainless steel rails. Because the team found that all cracks of this nature had occurred on the front of the rail only, an analysis was made to determine if the rear doublers were necessary. Since there were never any cracks observed on the rear of the rail, and the stress analysis did not indicate the necessity for the rear doublers, the team recommended that the rear doublers could be removed, which was a labor and material savings.

- The team researched the impact of two common weld-related defects, undercuts, and rollover welds, and found that in both cases, areas of stress concentrations develop that can contribute to the formation of cracks. The team estimated that the stress concentration factor for undercuts and rollover welds is 2.5 times the normal stress loads. Because of this fact (based upon the laws of physics), the team recommended that the operations areas in both plants must take preventive measures to reduce both of these welding defects.

- The team also studied the effect of a new design that, if implemented, would increase the fatigue safety factor from 0.82 for the standard configuration to 2.09 for the redesign, thus cutting the risk of another failure by more than two times. Having said this, by using the other recommended improvements (i.e., 1/4 inch mounting angle plus a 3/8 bend radius, plus a 1/4 inch mount doubler on the front of the rail only), provides a fatigue life safety factor of 2.04, which was nearly the same as the new rail design.

21.10 HYPOTHESIZE/TEST FOR POTENTIAL ROOT CAUSES

The team brainstormed and developed theories for the cracking problem and, where appropriate, developed additional tests to either validate or invalidate the theories. For each of the things the team knew to be true or believed to be true, it performed either stress analysis or some other physical measurement or observation to prove or disprove things from either list.

21.11 DEFINE THE MOST PROBABLE CAUSE(S)

Based upon the team's complete body of knowledge (i.e., causal chains, test results, distinctions, and changes), the team developed what we believed was the most probable cause(s). The team concluded that the most probable cause of the mounting rail cracking was the failure of the rail system design to be robust enough to account for the normal process variation, as is evidenced by the following:

1. The introduction of the ¼ inch rails appeared to have stopped the incidence of cracking on the stainless-steel rails. Stress analysis confirmed that the ¼ rail design change significantly reduced the stresses.
2. The ½ inch bend radius in plant A has been proven, through stress analysis, to be inferior to the ⅜ rail in plant B.
3. The introduction of doublers at both plant B and plant A significantly reduced the stresses on the weld.

All three of these findings point to the original design not being robust enough. In addition to the preceding findings, the team also determined that weld undercuts, rollover welds, and off-centering of the undercarriage create areas of high stress concentration, which when combined with the original design probably played a role in the cracking problem.

21.12 DEFINE AND IMPLEMENT CORRECTIONS AND CONTROLS

The next step in this problem-solving exercise was to implement the necessary corrections under controlled conditions, and then develop ways to never again permit the same root cause to be repeated. This is done by developing short- and long-term corrections and controls. In this team's case, most of the corrections had already been implemented in plant B and plant A, but the team believed that, based upon the results of a stress analysis, plant A must implement ⅜ bend radius as plant B had done.

In addition, both facilities developed an inspection method to reduce/ eliminate the incidence of undercuts, rollover welds, and off-centering of the undercarriage. In the short term, it was recommended that both facilities implement a visual inspection by either quality control or the supervisor.

One final control was developed and implemented at both facilities to prevent or substantially reduce the probability that nonrobust designs of any kind would be developed. Both facilities would make it mandatory that all designs be confirmed by rigorous stress analysis.

___

21.13 CELEBRATE AND DOCUMENT SUCCESS

The team concluded its problem-solving experience by documenting all that it had accomplished in a formal report that would serve as a guide for future teams to replicate and imitate. The team had become skilled at following a structured and systematic approach to problem solving and had achieved its objectives. And of course, the team members then celebrated!

22

The Case of the Weld Spatter

Whatever failures I have known, whatever errors I have committed, whatever follies I have witnessed in public and private life have been the consequences of action without thought.

Bernard Baruch

22.1 BACKGROUND INFORMATION

In this chapter we will discuss a case study that demonstrates how the use of a structured problem-solving process not only solved two chronic quality problems but also significantly impacted throughput within the same department. It is important to understand that oftentimes as we solve a problem, there are positive side benefits that we may or may not have been anticipating.

The company we will be studying is a manufacturer of stainless steel pressurized vessels used to hold a variety of liquids and gases. Sheets of stainless steel are rolled into tubes that are then welded together before structural rings are mounted and welded to the exterior of these large stainless steel tubes to provide the needed strength to counteract the applied pressures of the liquids and gases that are held and transported inside the tanks.

Two common problems encountered when welding products of this nature are pinholes and weld spatter. Weld spatter occurs when the welding arc virtually explodes and coats the surrounding area with bits of welding wire that must be ground off for aesthetic purposes. Pinholes are small cavity-type discontinuities formed by gas entrapment that can occur for a variety of reasons. Both of these defects are caused by many of the same reasons, so it was the general belief of this company that if it could solve the weld spatter problem, then pinholes would be reduced as well.

As the stainless steel support rings are welded into place, weld spatter forms along the entire diameter of the tank in close proximity to these structural rings. Removing the spatter takes significant time and, as such, had created a sizeable bottleneck in the normal process flow, which, in turn, had a negative impact on throughput. Actually, for a typical tank, the amount of time required to remove the weld spatter alone was averaging a bit over six hours.

22.2 THE STRUCTURED APPROACH

Like all other case studies presented in this book, the Problem Solving Roadmap was utilized to attack this problem. Figure 22.1 is the graphic of this approach.

22.3 DEFINE, DESCRIBE, AND APPRAISE THE PROBLEM

A team was formed that included members from the tank fabrication area, finishing where the rework is performed, quality assurance, design engineering, and finance to study ways to either eliminate or significantly reduce the most significant factors causing the extended time in finishing. The first deliverable in this approach is the creation of a problem statement, but before doing so, the team had many questions to answer.

Like nearly all of the companies that I go into, the development of a data collection system is usually the first action taken by the team. The team developed a simple system to rapidly collect information on all downtime and rework in the tank or barrel area. The team collected the downtime and rework data, and determined that during a period of approximately two weeks, weld-related defects around the structural rings accounted for approximately forty-two hours of rework in the tank finishing area. This accounted for about 40% of the total downtime hours. The breakdown of these repairs is as follows:

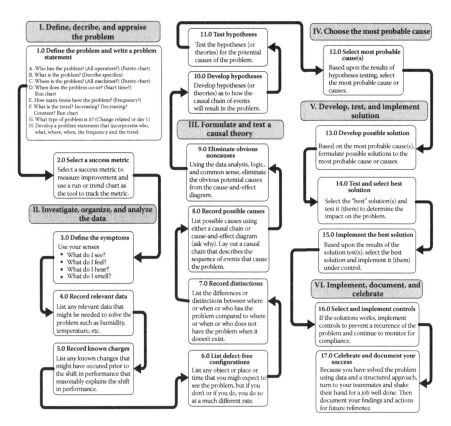

FIGURE 22.1
Problem Solving Roadmap.

Grind and chip spatter	20.25 hours
Weld pinholes and die test	14.5 hours
Weld pinholes	6.5 hours
Total	41.25 hours

Rework of this nature, is typically related to the actual welding process and equipment being used, but operator technique generally plays a significant role as well.

As I said, the approach used by this team was to follow the same Problem Solving Roadmap that I have demonstrated repeatedly throughout this book. As I have stated many times, it is crucial for problems of this nature that the team follow a structured approach, starting with the development of a problem statement, so that all members of the team understand the problem exactly the same. In order to do this, the following questions had to be answered:

1. *What?* What is the specific object with the performance problem, and what specifically on the object is considered to be the fault, defect, or performance problem? In this case study, the specific object was the stainless steel tanks, and the faults were pinholes and weld spatter, especially in the area of the external structural rings.
2. *Where?* Where is the object with the problem and where physically on the object is the defect or fault located? In this case study, the physical location was the company's tank finishing area, and the location on the tank was in close proximity to the external structural support rings.
3. *When?* When is the performance problem observed? That is, when, from a time perspective, and when in the life cycle of the object is the defect or fault seen? In our case study, the faults or defects were observed in the finishing area after the welding of the external support rings during inspection. It is important to note that since no historical data was available, the team could not be certain how long the problems with weld spatter and pinholes had actually existed. This fact is important, because the team could not associate this problem with a change and would, therefore, be considered as a launch-type problem, or a problem that had always existed to some degree.
4. *Scope?* What is the scope of the performance problem? That is, how many objects have the defect, and how much of the object is consumed with the defect? In our case study, 100% of the tanks produced had either weld spatter or pinholes or both primarily close to the structural rings.
5. *Trend?* What is the current rate of the performance problem and is the problem spreading to the remaining parts of the object? Is the performance problem increasing, decreasing, or remaining constant? The team evaluated the data it had collected and concluded that the trend was somewhat constant.

At this company, like so many others I have encountered, there was no automated system in place that would facilitate the retrieval of the defects (i.e., in this case, pinhole and weld spatter data). In the longer term, a defect or downtime database would have to be developed, but in the short term, a manual system was employed to collect the data. A simple Excel format using the current time cards was initiated to capture rework information by defect type and by shift, but it did not provide specific information on things like which operator might have caused the defect or where the defect was located, so the team elected to simply review each tank and manually assemble the information on location and welding operator.

Figure 22.2 is a Pareto chart of the data that this team assembled, and as you can easily discern, grind and chip spatter, and weld pinholes were the top two problems in the tank finishing (also referred to as the barrel area).

After reviewing Figure 22.2, the team had no trouble identifying and deciding upon which problems to attempt to solve. The data clearly told the team to attack both pinholes and weld spatter.

The team then collected weld spatter and pinhole rework hours for fifteen consecutive days, then plotted both on a run chart (see Figure 22.3). For the fifteen-day period, the combined rework hours for pinholes and weld spatter averaged approximately eleven hours per day for this time period. This run chart would serve as a baseline for improvement for this team and would be used as the team's success metric to measure progress against these two defects.

It is important to mention here that any time data collection is involved, we must be certain that the inspection system used to gather the data is calibrated appropriately, so that all of the inspectors amassing the data

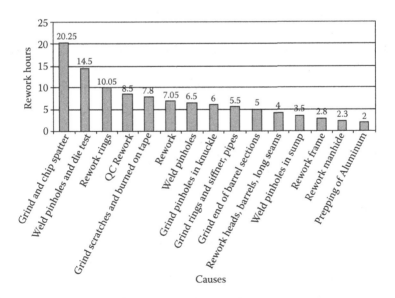

FIGURE 22.2
Pareto chart of rework by cause in barrel area.

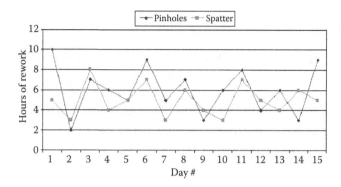

FIGURE 22.3
Daily weld spatter and pinholes rework hours.

are doing so in the same manner. This is especially important when the inspection entails a visual judgment against a predetermined standard. The team discussed this need to provide assurance that all inspectors would detect and classify the two defects in the same manner. Since no standard existed, the team had to develop one. To this end, a series of photos of the two defects that would serve as standards was developed. The photos were reviewed and classified independently by each inspector, and then the results were evaluated to determine the accuracy and precision of the inspection. Along with the photos, the team developed a visual rating system based on a scale of 1 to 10 to be used to determine if improvements had been made. The team implemented the new inspection criteria, which actually worked quite well.

Based upon the information collected and team discussions, the team agreed on the following problem statement:

> Pinholes and weld spatter are occurring on 100% of the stainless steel tanks, at a rate of approximately eleven hours per day on stainless steel tanks creating significant amounts of rework. Based upon a recent study, as much as 100 hours per week of rework time has been observed for these two problems, and the trend is constant.

Now that all members of the team understand the problem exactly the same, they can begin the process that will ultimately lead them to the root cause and corrective action. At the risk of being redundant, this step must be completed before the team can move forward in the problem-solving process.

22.4 INVESTIGATE, ORGANIZE, AND ANALYZE THE DATA

The next step for the team to accomplish was to investigate the problem, in much the same manner as a police force would investigate a crime. There are clues and bits of evidence at the scene of the crime that, when assembled in a logical and structured fashion, will lead the team of investigators to the root cause of these problems. So, the team investigated, organized, and then analyzed all of the pertinent and relevant information.

22.5 RECORD THE SYMPTOMS AND RELEVANT DATA

Symptoms are the warning signs and signals that something has gone out of kilter or amiss. Just as a doctor records things like, temperature, blood pressure, or visual abnormalities, so too must the team look for outward signs that things are not as they might be or should be. As a group, the team reviewed the process of making tanks, recorded various observations, and then met to discuss their findings as follows:

1. There was a noticeable and inconsistent gap between the tank and the structural rings prior to welding the rings in place. Where the gap existed, there was an excessive amount of weld spatter present.
2. Not all welders were operating at the same speed setting.
3. The tanks were located on variable speed, floor-mounted rollers that turned the tanks as the welds were made. The turning speeds were not the same for all tanks.
4. As the tanks turned on the rollers, oftentimes there would be a jerking or slipping action that tended to speed up and slow down the tanks during the welding of the rings.
5. The antispatter material used was not applied consistently by all the weld operators.
6. Not all welders were using the same welding wire type.
7. The welding angle used by the welders was inconsistent from operator to operator.
8. The legs on the rings did not appear to be symmetrical from side to side.

The team had done a wonderful job of reviewing the process and generating a list of symptoms, and I was certain that the list of symptoms would be valuable information as the team attempted to solve this problem.

22.6 RECORD RECENT CHANGES

The team searched for any changes that might have occurred that could have impacted the level of weld spatter or pinholes, but since no hard data had been recorded, the team was forced to interview other employees that had worked in the welding area for some time. The only known change was that several years prior the company had changed both the antispatter material and the method of dispensing it. The antispatter material had changed from a water-based material that was brushed onto the tanks to the material they are currently using. This change was done to reduce the amount of time required to apply the material. The current material permits the operators to spray it onto the tank. When asked if they remembered the impact on weld spatter, it was clear that some employees preferred the brush-on material, because they believed that they had less spatter, while others believed that the new method was superior. Since there was such a split in opinions, the team elected to test both types and application methods for the antispatter material. It did so and saw no difference between the two.

22.7 LIST DEFECT-FREE CONFIGURATIONS AND DISTINCTIONS

You will recall that a *defect-free configuration*, or DFC, is found by asking the question of where or when you would expect to see the problem, but you don't or you do but at a significantly less rate. The team evaluated the process and information it had collected and concluded that welding areas away from the structural rings could be considered as a DFC on the basis of the smaller amount of weld spatter and pinholes present in those locations.

Since the team was convinced that there was a defect-free configuration available, the next step was to search for and record any distinctions. The team weighed heavily on the list of symptoms and concluded that the gap between the tank and the structural rings was a clear distinction. The team noted that when there was a gap present, the weld operator was required to fill in the gap with weld wire. No other noticeable distinctions were found.

22.8 RECORD POSSIBLE CAUSES

The team was now ready to develop a list of potential causes for the weld spatter, so I gave them a choice of using a cause-and-effect diagram or causal chains to generate this list. After explaining how to use both tools, the team elected to use the causal chain technique.

As explained in other chapters, the causal chain begins with a statement of the problem, with the object on top of the line and the state that it is in directly beneath it. In this team's causal chain, the object was the weld spatter, with the state being that it is present. The team then, moving from right to left on the causal chains, asked the question why until it arrived at a potential root cause.

Figure 22.4 is the series of causal chains developed by this team, and as you can see, ten separate chains were developed. For example, one of the chains was related to the tank roller jerking. When the team asked why the tank roller was jerking, it was believed that the clutch could be worn out. When they subsequently asked why the clutch was worn out, the conclusion was that no preventive maintenance was in place.

For each of the ten individual chains, the team continued in the same manner as this example, until it arrived at a potential root cause. The team had, once again, grasped the essence of this exercise and completed the step to perfection.

22.9 ELIMINATE OBVIOUS NONCAUSES

The next step for the team was to eliminate causes that it believed were not relevant to the problem of weld spatter or pinholes. As it turned out, most of the causes listed in the causal chains were legitimate and would result in actions being taken. The only potential cause that the team actually

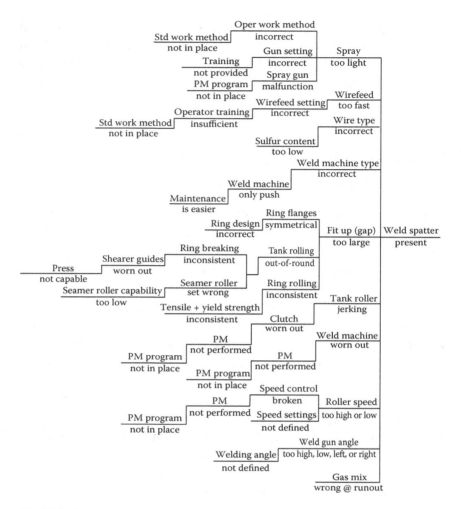

FIGURE 22.4
Causal chain for weld spatter.

eliminated was the gas mix being wrong at run-out. The others were all seen as process deficiencies that required actions to correct them. For example, it was clear that the company needed a preventive maintenance program, so the team created a simple, operator-based preventive maintenance program to avoid some of these problems in the future. In addition, it was clear that welding training was a problem, so the team contacted the manufacturer of the welding machines, who graciously agreed to hold training classes free of charge.

22.10 DEVELOP AND TEST HYPOTHESES

The team narrowed the list to a single potential root cause. The team deduced that the tank to ring gap problem, which had been earlier recorded as a symptom, was probably the factor that contributed the most to weld spatter generation, but it needed to develop a theory as to why the gap was present and it did.

The team worked backward through the process to better understand why the gap problem existed. It checked the roundness and concentricity of the tanks, and found that there was not a strong correlation between concentricity of the tank, and presence of gaps, so this step in the process was eliminated. The team next looked at the process that produces the structural rings. The ring material is first sheared into rectangular pieces, sent to a bender to create supposedly symmetrical legs, before the pieces are sent to a rolling machine, where they are rolled into circular rings.

The team first looked at the completed rings and found that the legs were neither equal nor consistent in length. The team believed that these two observations could explain the gap, but in order to develop a logical cause-and-effect theory, the team had to find the cause of the inequality and inconsistency of the ring legs. The team investigated the rolling process first and concluded that the problems with the ring legs were not created at the roller, but could be aggravated during the rolling process.

The team then reviewed the bending process and noted that the material coming to the bender was already asymmetrical, so the bending process was not the source of the problem. The team then reviewed the shearing process and found the source of the asymmetry immediately. The guides were badly worn, which then presented the sheets of steel to the bender askew, causing the parts to be seriously out of square. The team now had a good idea of what had caused the problem with asymmetrical rings.

Knowing this information, the team developed its hypothesis as to why weld spatter was so prevalent in proximity to the structural rings. The gap was, of course, the underlying cause of the weld spatter, but the cause of the gap was the real root cause. Since the shear machine was producing asymmetrical parts (i.e., up to a half-inch difference in width from one end to the other) when the rings were mounted on the tanks, a gap was created that had to be filled with excess amounts of weld wire. The excess weld wire set the stage for weld spatter to form.

22.11 DEVELOP, TEST, AND IMPLEMENT SOLUTIONS

Because the team was convinced that if it could fix the asymmetry, the gap would be corrected, then, therefore, weld spatter would be reduced. The team had the worn guides replaced and had a total preventive maintenance effort of the shear machine done. The team had parts produced and all were found to be acceptable. Just to be certain, the team followed the parts through the bending and rolling process, and found the parts to be symmetrical and consistent from end to end. The team then followed the parts through the tank area and observed no gap when they were mounted on the tanks. Finally, the team observed the rings being welded in place on the tanks, and to the team's delight, the incidence of weld spatter was significantly reduced.

22.12 IMPLEMENT, DOCUMENT, AND CELEBRATE

The team had solved the biggest problem causing weld spatter, but as happy as the team was with the results, the team knew that unless it developed some sort of control for squareness that the problem would return. The team needed to develop a control that would guarantee that the two most important factors—width and squareness of the parts going to the bender—would remain in control. The tool the team chose to accomplish this was a control chart, as seen in Figure 22.5. The team collected data for two weeks and then developed a control chart. Training was provided to the shear machine operators, and the problem was resolved. Figure 22.6 is the run chart of weld spatter and pinholes that the team had developed as its success metric, and as you can readily see, pinhole repair hours decreased from an average of approximately 6 hours per day to about 45 minutes per day. At the same time, weld spatter decreased from approximately 5¼ hours to about 30 minutes per day. In total, the team had taken two defects averaging approximately 11½ hours per day to about 1½ hours or an approximate 87% decrease.

The team concluded its problem-solving activities by documenting what they had done in a formal report, and then made a formal presentation to the management team. The magnitude of what this team had accomplished

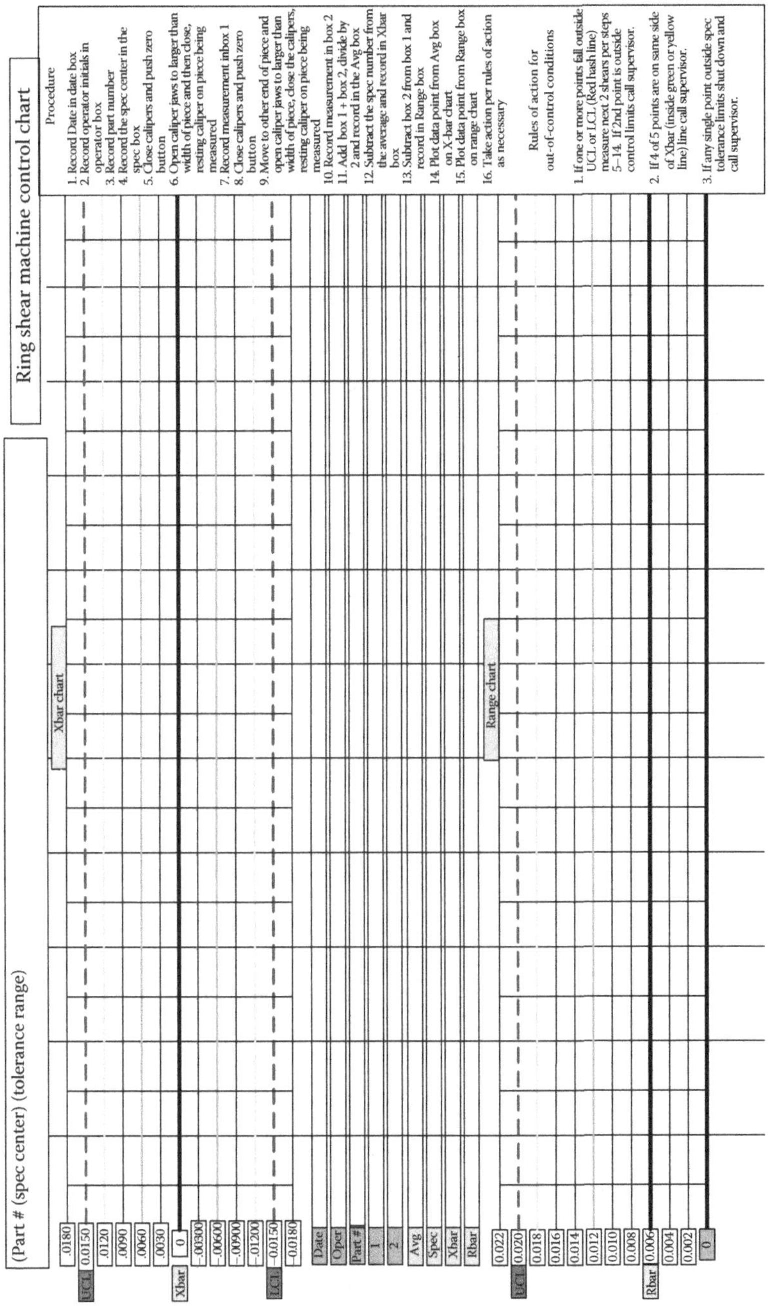

Ring shear machine control chart

(Part # (spec center) (tolerance range)

Xbar chart

Range chart

Procedure

1. Record Date in date box
2. Record operator initials in operator box
3. Record part number
4. Record the spec center in the spec box
5. Close calipers and push zero button
6. Open caliper jaws to larger than width of piece and then close, resting caliper on piece being measured
7. Record measurement in box 1
8. Close calipers and push zero button
9. Move to other end of piece and open caliper jaws to larger than width of piece, close the calipers, resting caliper on piece being measured
10. Record measurement in box 2
11. Add box 1 + box 2, divide by 2 and record in the Avg box
12. Subtract the spec number from the average and record in Xbar box
13. Subtract box 2 from box 1 and record in Range box
14. Plot data point from Avg box on X-bar chart
15. Plot data point from Range box on range chart
16. Take action per rules of action as necessary

Rules of action for out-of-control conditions

1. If one or more points fall outside UCL or LCL (Red hash line) measure next 2 shears per steps 5–14. If 2nd point is outside control limits call supervisor.
2. If 4 of 5 points are on same side of Xbar (inside green or yellow line) line call supervisor.
3. If any single point outside spec tolerance limits shut down and call supervisor.

.0180
UCL 0.0150
.0120
.0090
.0060
.0030
Xbar 0
-.0030
-.0060
-.0090
-.0120
LCL -0.0150
-.0180

Date
Oper
Part #
1
2
Avg
Spec
Xbar
Rbar

0.022
UCL 0.020
0.018
0.016
0.014
0.012
0.010
0.008
Rbar 0.006
0.004
0.002
0

FIGURE 22.5
Control chart.

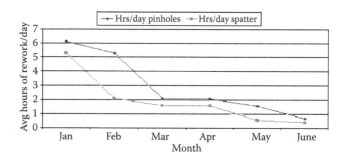

FIGURE 22.6

Weld spatter and pinholes average daily rework by month.

was simply overwhelming to the leadership of this plant. Once again, this team of very ordinary employees had achieved very extraordinary things by simply following a structured and systematic approach as outlined in the Problem Solving Roadmap. The problem-solving team and the management team celebrated!

23

A Case Study in Problem Prevention

Difficulties are opportunities to better things; they are stepping-stones to greater experience. ... When one door closes, another always opens; as a natural law it has to, to balance.

Brian Adams

23.1 CASE BACKGROUND

One of the responsibilities and obligations of leadership in any organization is to look into the future, see it, understand it, and then make plans to protect it. The leadership of an organization has the authority and influence to walk into the future, find potential areas of risk and vulnerability, and then do something about them now in the present to either prevent the problems from occurring, or mitigate and neutralize their effects if they were to occur. In this case study, we will look at a company that hadn't spent much time examining and analyzing the future, so this was new for it. But even though the company had not peered into the future before, it was able to learn simple techniques to do so, and what it found and ultimately accomplished was nothing short of remarkable.

Our case study involves a company that makes plastic bottles used to hold a variety of liquids, including spring water and soft drinks. Its current process produced bottles at rates approaching 200 bottles per minute. This company's bottle sales were sluggish and somewhat stagnant, and it was searching for new markets to penetrate. Sales hadn't met targets in the past two years, so after much internal debate, the company decided to use the services of someone outside the company who was unbiased.

When I arrived at the company, it was evident to me that it was looking for some miracle cure for its lackluster sales. The CEO of the company introduced me to his senior managers and told them that I was here to "fix" the problem with sales. As the executive in charge of sales introduced himself, it was clear to me that he was not happy that I was there and that he was not about to welcome me with open arms. I assumed that he viewed me as some sort of threat or risk who would ultimately make him appear incompetent.

The CEO had asked each member of his team to prepare a brief presentation of their future plans for the company in their own sphere of expertise. Marketing elucidated its plans to push a new product line that, to me, seemed like just a smarter version of already existing products. Maintenance presented its plans to install a bigger, better, and faster, high-speed bottling machine that would produce 30% more bottles than the fastest machine the company now had. One by one, each department presented its future plans.

At the end of their presentations, the CEO turned to me and wanted to know what I thought about what I had heard. I told him that his staff appeared to be quite competent and seemed like they knew their jobs well, but that I was confused. I told them that I hadn't heard any plans that would lead me to believe that sales would increase. A hush came over the conference room and all eyes were on me. When I asked them how any of their plans they had presented would increase sales, the silence was deafening. I asked the CEO and his staff how they had arrived at each of their particular projects, and why they believed that their lackluster sales were their most pressing problem. They told me that they had each come up with their plans by themselves, just as they do every year as part of the annual budget process. I asked them again, "Which of the projects, if any, would increase sales? And why is increasing sales so important?" This time I got responses like, "Every company needs sales" or "We always have a plan to increase our sales for the next year." Then I asked them, "But what if sales, isn't your most pressing issue?" I told them that they needed to put their projects on hold, at least until we took the time to look into the future.

23.2 A STRUCTURED APPROACH TO PROBLEM PREVENTION

Two things struck me after that first meeting. First, they apparently hadn't considered their future needs or areas of risk as a group; and second, except for the maintenance plan, their plans lacked continuity, with respect to what they believed was the most urgent and pressing problem facing their company, sales. At least the maintenance executive, had anticipated a sales increase, and developed a plan to produce more products.

In light of my observations in that first meeting, the next day I reassembled the staff and presented the Problem Prevention Roadmap (Figure 23.1) as a way of looking into the future, anticipating any areas that might be at risk, prioritizing them, and then developing a *preventive measures plan*. The series of meetings that followed with the CEO and his staff proved to be a very valuable exercise for this team.

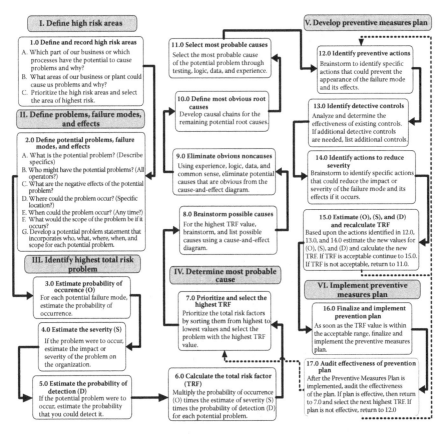

FIGURE 23.1
Problem Prevention Roadmap.

23.3 DEFINING HIGH-RISK AREAS

The first action an organization must accomplish is an unbiased look into the future to identify any areas where the organization might be vulnerable or where a planned activity might fail. This glimpse into the future can be a broad review of the entire organization, looking at things like how a major competitor could attempt to attack the company's market position or simply a review of a project already scheduled for implementation, to find obstacles or complications that might prevent the smooth and timely completion of the project. Whatever the case, the roadmap is intended to identify what could or might go wrong, and what the impact might be on the organization or project. As a result of this look, potential problems will be identified that necessitate the development of plans that will either prevent the potential negative effects of the problem or mitigate the negative effects if the problem can't be prevented. Unlike the negative aura surrounding existing problems, predicting the future should be treated as a positive event.

It is sometimes difficult to get a group talking about the future, because as long as performance and profit margins are good, and the board of directors is happy, then there is a feeling of invincibility and supremacy. To a certain extent, organizations become complacent and indifferent toward the future, because everything in the present is good. It's sort of, "If it ain't broke, don't fix it," kind of attitude. This group of executives was no different in that it took a full hour to break them away from their apparent comfort zone of the present. Finally, near the end of the first hour, the maintenance executive chimed in and said that he was concerned that the installation of the new, high-speed bottling machine wouldn't be ready to run when it was supposed to. His comment seemed to break the ice, as the vice president of sales expressed his concern about missing his sales targets for a third straight year. When the session ended, the team had developed a sizeable list of potential areas of vulnerability or areas of high risk.

Now that the team had this list, I explained to them that although the list was a good list, there were simply too many potential problems and that we needed to whittle the list down to something more manageable. There are several ways to reshape this list, but the most uncomplicated and straightforward way is to consider the consequences if the planned activity or the future concern was to happen against the chances of it happening.

These consequences can be thought of in terms of lost revenue, loss of market share, impact on customer base, and so on. For each future issue this team had raised, I told them to consider and rate the chances that it will occur against the negative consequences to the organization if it does occur. For example, it would make very little sense to spend much time constructing a plan to counteract something that has a low chance of happening with low consequences. On the other hand, items that have a high chance of happening with elevated negative consequences must be considered. Keep one thing in mind when you are sorting your list of could-be problems. This is a view from 10,000 feet, so we are not using exact probability numbers to determine probability of occurrence and severity. We are only trying to sort out the potential problems that could be a legitimate risk to the company.

Figure 23.2 is a simple tool I presented to the team to help it narrow its list to the top two or three items to consider. The red blocks (the blocks are labeled Red, Yellow, and Green) indicate the potential problems of greatest concern, while the green shaded blocks indicate problems that are of

		Consequences		
		Low	Medium	High
Chances of occurring	Low	Green	Green Labor unrest by union over wages or benefits.	Yellow
	Medium	Green Sales misses budgeted volume increase.	Yellow Outside maintenance company goes out of business.	Red The installation of the new high-speed bottling machine won't be completed on schedule.
	High	Yellow	Red The attempt by our number one bottle competitor to seal our market share.	Red Resin supplier either cannot supply additional raw material or the cost of raw materials skyrockets due to oil shortage.

FIGURE 23.2
Chances of occurring versus consequences matrix.

lower concern. Red blocks have a medium or high chance of occurring, and medium or high impact on the organization.

The team reviewed its list of concerns and debated the chances of the potential problem occurring against the negative consequences on the organization if the potential problems were to occur. Since the object of this exercise is to compare the concerns against one another, it was relatively easy to force fit each one into a box.

After much discussion and disagreement, the team of executives had whittled its list to the following three future concerns:

1. The installation of the new, high-speed bottling machine not being completed on schedule.
2. The attempt by their number one competitor to steal market share from them.
3. Resin supplier either cannot supply enough or additional raw material, or the cost of raw materials skyrockets due to oil shortages.

The team then evaluated each of these final three concerns and decided by simply using logic and their experience that the concern over resin supply would be the issue of greatest impact on the organization. The team reasoned that if resin could not be supplied in adequate volumes, then the concern over the installation of the new high-speed bottling machine would become a moot point. That is, there would be no need to even install the new machine. Likewise, a shortage of resin or a spike in the price of oil would not only affect their own company's ability to produce and ship bottles, but their competitors would be equally affected. As it turned out, this was an excellent decision, because eight months later, the price of crude oil did spike dramatically, and shortages of resin were a common occurrence.

23.4 DEFINING PROBLEMS, FAILURE MODES, AND EFFECTS

Now that the team had prioritized and finalized its list, it was now ready to begin the problem prevention assignment by answering the questions in Box 2.0 of the Problem Prevention Roadmap, as follows:

1. *What is the potential problem?* As stated earlier, the potential problem is the inability of the resin supplier to supply enough raw material or the cost of raw materials skyrockets due to oil shortages. I explained to the team members that they had mixed two potential problems together. On one hand, they were worried about whether the resin supplier could supply enough raw materials to support their growth plan, while on the other hand if the cost of the raw material significantly increased, then sales could be negatively impacted. On one hand, they were concerned about not being able to supply enough bottles compared to their cost to produce bottles that would create a condition whereby sales might decrease. Again, the team members logically concluded that the concern over not enough raw materials was potentially more serious than the cost increase, so they chose the former over the latter.
2. *Who might have the potential problem?* From an internal perspective, the potential lack of raw material could impact all machines. From a market perspective, the problem would most likely impact all companies producing bottles.
3. *What are the negative effects of the potential problem?* The team brainstormed and produced the following list of negative effects of a raw material shortage:
   a. Inability to meet the needs of our customer base.
   b. Our reputation within the industry will be damaged.
   c. Customers will move to other suppliers.
   d. Without additional raw material, our planned production and corresponding sales increase would fail.
4. *Where could the problem occur?* The team again brainstormed and concluded that the problem could occur on all product lines that used this particular raw material, which, in this case was 80% of the bottles produced.
5. *When could the problem occur?* The team concluded that the problem could occur at any time in the future, but especially after an announcement by OPEC (Organization of Petroleum Exporting Countries) to reduce its output of oil, and could last indefinitely.
6. *What would the scope of the problem be if it does occur?* The team discussed the scope of this problem if it were to occur, and agreed that it would impact all customers, except the ones who receive bottles made of a non-oil-based resin.

The team was now ready to formulate its *potential problem statement* using all of the answers to the questions it had just answered and it did so as follows: "At any time in the future (but especially if OPEC announces a cutback of oil supply), there could be a shortage of oil-based resin to produce enough bottles, which could negatively affect 80% of our customers."

In this case study, the identification of potential failure modes was not a difficult assignment. The team brainstormed again and created a list of potential failure modes that could lead to the potential problem of reduced oil-based resin. The list was as follows:

1. OPEC announces a significant reduction in oil production that would, in turn, impact our resin supplier's ability to produce resin in sufficient quantities, which would limit our output of bottles.
2. Our major supplier has a catastrophic accident (fire, explosion, etc.) that would suddenly terminate all shipments of oil-based resin, which would significantly reduce our output of bottles.
3. Pending federal regulations on oil-based resin are approved, making it difficult for our suppliers to produce and ship enough resin to us, which, in turn, would reduce our output of bottles to 80% of our customers.
4. Terrorists strike a series of American oil refineries, virtually shutting down refinement of oil, which would shut down the supply of materials needed to produce resin at our supplier.
5. A labor dispute at our supplier shuts down production of resin, which, in turn, stops our own production of bottles using oil-based resin.
6. The predicted growth of China's and India's economies creates a worldwide shortage of oil.
7. A war in the Middle East virtually shuts down production of a significant amount of oil, which limits how much resin our supplier can produce and ship to us.
8. A significant weather event, such as a hurricane, earthquake, tornado, or flood, would either destroy the supplier's facility or temporarily interrupt the supply of resin.

Now that the team had identified the failure modes that could lead to a shortage of oil-based resin, it was time to evaluate each for probability of occurrence, severity, and the company's ability to detect the problem either prior to it happening or immediately after.

23.5 IDENTIFY THE HIGHEST TOTAL RISK PROBLEM

Creating a list of potential problems is not that difficult, but being able to determine the likelihood that it will occur, the negative impact on the organization, and the probability of detection are a bit more tedious. Think about it; we are peering into the future and trying to estimate whether a potential problem might occur. Calculating the impact on the organization is equally difficult, since we aren't sure about the depth of the problem. Will the problem occur exactly as we think it will, or will it occur at some percentage of what it could be? And how will we know when the problem occurs? Will we receive enough advance warning, or will we suddenly have the problem? These are all points to ponder as we try to prioritize the potential problems.

23.6 ESTIMATE THE PROBABILITY OF OCCURRENCE, SEVERITY, AND DETECTION

Estimating the probability that a specific event will occur, and the impact on the organization, is not always an easy task, especially if it involves factors beyond your control, like a shortage of incoming raw materials. The team knew that there were several potential reasons that this might happen, so it was time to estimate how probable it was that any of these causes might occur and then estimate how the problem might impact the company. For example, if the oil-based resin shortage is caused by an OPEC decision to cut oil production, the team knew it had no control over whether this was going to happen. On the other hand, if there was a fire at the supplier location, for example, a review of the company's safety program and history of fires within the plant would be available, so real data could be used to estimate the probability of this happening.

Table 23.1 is a simple Excel spreadsheet that the team developed to evaluate each of the potential failure modes for occurrence, severity, and detection. The team will consider all that is known about each failure mode and seek additional information as needed to estimate as accurately as possible. Keep in mind that detection, in this scenario, is the probability that this company will find a trigger to alert it of any impending trouble

TABLE 23.1

Matrix of Occurrence, Severity, and Detection

Failure Mode	Occurrence (O)	Severity (S)	Detection (D)	Total Risk Factor (TRF)	Action Item	New (O)	New (S)	New (D)	New TRF
OPEC announces cutback									
Catastrophic accident									
Federal regulation change									
Terrorist strike									
Labor strike at supplier									
China's and India's economies									
Middle East war									
Catastrophic weather event									

far enough in advance to be able to implement the appropriate portion of its prevention plan.

23.7 ESTIMATE THE PROBABILITY OF OCCURRENCE

One by one the team discussed each of the seven failure modes and using a scale of 1 to 10 rated the probability of occurrence of each of the failure modes. At times, the debate was heated, as each executive presented his or her opinions on how likely each failure mode was to occur. Table 23.2 includes the final consensus.

As each item was debated, it became more apparent that very few of the failure modes the team had developed were within their scope of control. As a matter of fact, only the catastrophic accident, the potential labor strike at the company's resin supplier, and federal regulation changes were the only three failure modes that the team could impact, and their impact would be only superficial. This was troubling to the team members, but I reminded them that their problem prevention plan had three parts: prevention, contingency plans to lessen the impact, and being able to detect the failure in time. For those failure modes that they either had limited or no potential to influence, their plan must be heavy into mitigating the severity or impact on the organization.

23.8 ESTIMATE THE SEVERITY

Once agreement and consensus was reached on how likely each of the potential failures might occur, it was time to discuss and agree upon how each of the failure modes might impact the capability to receive enough resin to produce and ship an adequate number of bottles in the event that any of the failure modes were to actually occur.

The team reasoned that the four failure modes that would have the most negative impact on the company were the three that would suddenly stop all shipments of resin to the company. A catastrophic accident such as an explosion or fire, a labor dispute that causes a strike, or a weather event could all immediately terminate all shipments of resin. The two lowest rated failure modes were China's and India's economies and a Middle East war;

TABLE 23.2

Matrix of Occurrence, Severity, and Detection with Occurrence

Failure Mode	Occurrence (O)	Severity (S)	Detection (D)	Total Risk Factor (TRF)	Action Item	New (O)	New (S)	New (D)	New TRF
OPEC announces cutback	7								
Catastrophic accident	5								
Federal regulation change	6								
Terrorist strike	5								
Labor strike at supplier	4								
China's and India's economies	9								
Middle East war	7								
Catastrophic weather event	5								

they were rated low because their impact would not be felt immediately. Table 23.3 includes the final ranking for each of the eight failure modes.

23.9 ESTIMATE THE PROBABILITY OF DETECTION

The final bit of information needed to be able to calculate the total risk factor for each of the potential failure modes is our ability to detect the failure mode occurring. Again, detection in this scenario means the likelihood that the team would have enough advanced warning (i.e., a trigger) to be able to successfully implement the corresponding portion of the preventive measures plan. A high number for detection indicates that the likelihood of detection is very low.

Table 23.4 contains the final detection numbers that were, at times, fiercely and emotionally debated. Everyone agreed that a catastrophic accident, a terrorist strike, and a catastrophic weather event were virtually undetectable until they occur, so they rated them all as a nine. The lower numbers (e.g., China's and India's economic growth) suggested that there would be enough advance warning to implement those portions of the plan.

The failure mode most passionately debated was the potential regulation change, because some of the members of the team believed that an appropriate lobbying effort could delay passage.

Having completed the estimates of occurrence, severity, and detection, it was now time to calculate the total risk factor (TRF) for each of the failure modes. The TRF will prioritize each of the failure modes for the team.

23.10 CALCULATE THE TOTAL RISK FACTOR (TRF)

Calculating the TRF is done by simply multiplying the probability of occurrence (O) times the severity (S) times the probability of detection (D), as follows:

$$TRF = O \times S \times D$$

The team did so and entered the results into the appropriate box in Table 23.5.

TABLE 23.3

Matrix of Occurrence, Severity, and Detection with Occurrence and Severity

Failure Mode	Occurrence (O)	Severity (S)	Detection (D)	Total Risk Factor (TRF)	Action Item	New (O)	New (S)	New (D)	New TRF
OPEC announces cutback	7	7							
Catastrophic accident	5	9							
Federal regulation change	6	8							
Terrorist strike	5	7							
Labor strike at supplier	4	9							
China's and India's economies	9	5							
Middle East war	7	5							
Catastrophic weather event	5	9							

TABLE 23.4

Matrix of Occurrence, Severity, and Detection with Occurrence, Severity, and Detection

Failure Mode	Occurrence (O)	Severity (S)	Detection (D)	Total Risk Factor (TRF)	Action Item	New (O)	New (S)	New (D)	New TRF
OPEC announces cutback	7	7	5						
Catastrophic accident	5	9	9						
Federal regulation change	6	8	5						
Terrorist strike	5	7	9						
Labor strike at supplier	4	9	7						
China's and India's economies	9	5	3						
Middle East war	7	5	4						
Catastrophic weather event	5	9	9						

TABLE 23.5

Matrix of Occurrence, Severity, and Detection with TRF Calculated

Failure Mode	Occurrence (O)	Severity (S)	Detection (D)	Total Risk Factor (TRF)	Action Item	New (O)	New (S)	New (D)	New TRF
OPEC announces cutback	7	7	5	245					
Catastrophic accident	8	9	9	648					
Federal regulation change	6	8	5	240					
Terrorist strike	5	7	9	315					
Labor strike at supplier	4	9	7	252					
China's and India's economies	9	5	3	135					
Middle East war	7	5	4	140					
Catastrophic weather event	5	9	9	405					

23.11 PRIORITIZE AND SELECT THE HIGHEST TRF

Each of the eight potential failure modes had been evaluated by the team, and in doing so, it became clear to the team that the single failure mode that it must develop a preventive measures plan for was a catastrophic accident at the resin supplier's factory. Selecting this failure mode does not suggest that all of the others can or should be ignored, but rather it simply indicates that this should be the team's primary area of focus, as the preventive measures plan is developed. This particular failure mode had the highest probability of occurrence, could have a severe impact on the organization, and would occur with no advance warning.

23.12 DETERMINE THE MOST PROBABLE CAUSE

The team was now ready to develop the most probable cause for this failure mode, and then proceed to develop actions that could either prevent the problem from occurring or mitigate the negative effects of the problem if it were to materialize. In addition, the team members would attempt to improve their ability to detect the problem if it were to occur.

The team brainstormed possible causes, eliminated obvious noncauses, and selected what it believe were the two most probable causes. Because the team felt strongly that it knew the two primary causes, it dispensed of preparing a cause-and-effect diagram and went directly to the development of the chain of events that could cause a catastrophic accident.

Figure 23.3 shows the causal chains developed by the team to answer the question of why a catastrophic accident might occur at the resin supplier. There were two potential primary causes that the team believed could result in a catastrophic accident. The first and most likely potential cause was the plant's already high accident rate. The team knew that the safety director had resigned in protest over the company's lack of concern for safety, and since then the accident rate had increased dramatically. The other potential cause of a catastrophe at the resin supplier was the supplier's lack of an effective preventive measures plan. Without effective preventive measures in place, the team feared that the resin supplier could have an explosion in one or more of the resin reactors used to make resin. If this did take place, it would take months to get the production line back in place, and in the

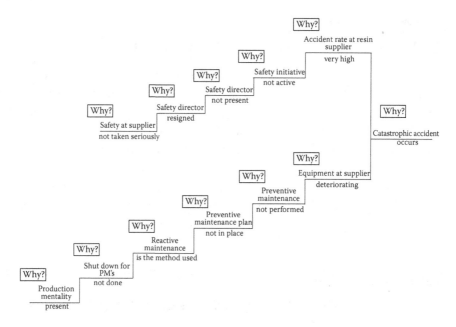

FIGURE 23.3
Causal chain of catastrophic accident occurring

interim, resin shortages would occur. With the most probable causes in place, the team was now ready to develop actions that could either prevent or mitigate the negative effects of the problem. After doing so, the team will reestimate O, S, and D, and then recalculate the total risk factor to estimate the effect of its actions on the potential problem.

23.13 DEVELOP PREVENTIVE MEASURES PLAN

The team members were feeling good about all they had done so far. They had identified future potential at-risk areas of their business; created a list of potential problems and the negative effects that go with them; and then prioritized the problems by estimating the probability of occurrence, the severity, and their ability to detect the event if it happens. Now it was time to brainstorm actions that will either reduce the chances of the negative event happening or, if it were to happen, minimize or lessen the impact on the organization. In addition, the team will look for ways to either know, in advance, that the problem is about to occur, or be alerted immediately after it does occur. This "trigger" will alert the team, so that its plan can be activated. These three actions represent the essence of an effective preventive measures plan.

23.14 IDENTIFY PREVENTIVE ACTIONS

The first step in the development of the preventive measures plan is to identify actions that are intended to either totally prevent or reduce the likelihood of occurrence of the problem. The team members discussed their options and concluded that one of the courses of action should be to meet with their current resin supplier, and be resolute that the supplier first implement an effective safety program that leadership solidly backs, and second develop a preventive measures plan that reduces the possibility of a catastrophic breakdown of their reactors. The team had identified both of these as potential root causes for a catastrophic accident that would prevent the supplier from shipping product.

The team members also discussed a contingency plan in the event the current supplier balked at their offer of assistance. Some members of the team felt it was time to move to another resin supplier, but in the end, it was decided that if their current supplier of resin did not agree to enhance its safety and preventive measures initiatives, then they would begin certification of a new resin supplier.

The second action was more long term in nature. The team made the decision that it was time to move away from the company's reliance on an oil-based resin and further develop the process that produces bottles made from non-oil-based resin. Since twenty percent of their current bottles were already produced with this type resin, the team concluded that this move would eliminate some of the other potential problems that were contingent upon the use of oil-based resin. In addition, much of the normal research and development work had already been done, so it was mostly a question of developing capacity, and convincing current customers that this was a better bottle.

23.15 IDENTIFY ACTIONS TO REDUCE SEVERITY

Although the next step in the roadmap was to develop controls that would give advance warning of the potential problem, the team elected to brainstorm and develop ways to reduce the impact on the organization if the resin supply chain was suddenly broken. The question that had to be answered was if the resin supply was suddenly terminated, how long would the supply stoppage last. An in-house inventory was taken, and it was found that a one-month supply was normally on hand.

The team met with the company's resin supplier to discuss the entire situation. Together, the supplier and the team concluded that if an accident were to happen that the resin supplier should have a safety stock of three months on hand to guard against a complete shutdown of the facility. Further, it was decided that until the supplier put in place an effective safety and preventive measures program, the storage of resin would be done so at a remote location. The team also agreed to pay half of the cost of the off-site storage. The team then added an incentive that if the resin supplier would rapidly implement effective safety and preventive measures programs, then it could reduce the amount of safety stock and even eliminate the off-site storage.

As one final motivation to take safety and maintenance seriously, the team discussed plans to potentially certify another supplier. The good news is that the supplier ensured the team that it would do everything required to remain their sole supplier of resin, and that it would immediately begin to work on ways to increase its capacity to produce non-oil-based resin.

23.16 IDENTIFY DETECTIVE CONTROLS

The final piece of the preventive measures plan is to identify ways to be able to detect, either in advance or as soon as possible, the onset of a problem. In this case, the team members felt that if they were intimately involved in the development of effective safety and preventive measures initiatives, then they could audit the supplier routinely for compliance. In doing so, the team members believed that they would have some degree of control over whether the supplier was seriously implementing these initiatives or just paying lip service to keep its status as the sole supplier of resin. The team met with the supplier, developed an implementation plan with a timeline, and prescheduled audits with specific milestones. Although the team would have liked to have guaranteed controls in place, these actions would be an adequate and satisfactory compromise.

TABLE 23.6

Completed Matrix

Failure Mode	Occurrence (O)	Severity (S)	Detection (D)	Total Risk Factor (TRF)	Action Item	New (O)	New (S)	New (D)	New TRF
OPEC announces cutback	7	7	5	245	Safety program and PM program	7	6	5	210
Catastrophic accident	8	9	9	648	Safety program and PM program	6	6	6	216
Federal regulation change	6	8	5	240	Safety program and PM program	6	8	5	240
Terrorist strike	5	7	9	315	Safety program and PM program	5	6	9	270
Labor strike at supplier	4	9	7	252	Safety program and PM program	4	6	6	144
China's and India's economies	9	5	3	135	Safety program and PM program	9	5	3	135
Middle East war	7	5	4	140	Safety program and PM program	7	5	4	140
Catastrophic weather event	5	9	9	405	Safety program and PM program	5	6	9	270

Note: PM, preventive measures.

23.17 ESTIMATE OCCURRENCE, SEVERITY, AND DETECTION, THEN RECALCULATE THE TRF

Now that the team had (1) developed actions that should reduce the likelihood that a sudden shortage of resin would occur, and if a shortage occurred, the team felt comfortable that it had (2) developed plans that would mitigate the impact on the company and customers, and (3) developed controls to know somewhat in advance of the potential problem, it was time to reestimate O, S, and D, and then calculate the new TRF.

Table 23.6 includes the new values for O, S, and D plus the TRF values. As you can see, the value for total risk factor related to a catastrophic accident at the supplier location improved from 648 to 216. As a matter of fact, most all of the TRFs improved with the plan that the team had created. The exceptions were the concern over the pending federal regulation change, China's and India's economic growth, and a catastrophic weather event. All three were beyond the scope of this team's sphere of influence.

23.18 FINALIZE, IMPLEMENT, AND AUDIT THE PREVENTIVE MEASURES PLAN

The team spent the next week finalizing and putting the finishing touches on its preventive measures plan. At the last moment, the team even decided to lobby the federal government to not implement the pending legislation change. The team had looked into the future, found potential problems with negative effects, and developed a plan that would reduce the chances of the most serious problems from happening. And in the event that the problems did occur, it put actions in place to minimize the impact on the company.

Although the catastrophic accident or weather event did not occur, and the regulation change didn't pass into law, and no terrorist attacks happened, the team learned the value of planning for the future. But the most important lesson of all for this team was the belief that organizations can impact the course of future events.

24

Decisions, Decisions, Decisions

In any moment of decision, the best thing you can do is the right thing, the next best thing is the wrong thing, and the worst thing you can do is nothing.

Theodore Roosevelt

24.1 MAKING CHOICES

Every day in life, one thing that is almost certain is that we will be called on to make a choice between different alternatives. We start each weekday deciding whether we will get up and go to work, what to wear, what to eat for breakfast, and when to leave for work. Fortunately for us, these decisions are simple and instinctive decisions and, as such, are undemanding and uncomplicated. As we move through the day at our jobs, the decisions and choices we make become more complex and difficult. Each of our decisions involve deciding what it is that we need and want, imagining alternatives that will supply our needs and wants, evaluating any risks and consequences that might arise, and then making a choice. Soon after we choose, we begin wondering if our choice of alternatives was correct. We worry until the results of our decision come to light, and when they do, we usually find out right away if we have made the right decision or the wrong decision.

For many, decisions are stressful, but do they really have to be? The answer is no they do not. Making difficult decisions can actually be accomplished with little or no worry if we simply follow a structured and systematic process. I'm sure by now you've noticed that in both problem prevention and problem solving, there were decisions that needed to be made. Deciding which solution for a problem or choosing which area of your company is the highest risk area. Just like the roadmaps for problem solving and prevention, effective decision making will only result from following the structured and systematic approach like the one presented in Figure 24.1, the *Decision Making Roadmap.*

There are six major sections in the roadmap, all signifying a separate purpose and function. The six sections of the roadmap are

1. Create a Statement of Purpose
2. Define the Criteria for the Decision
3. Develop a List of Potential Options
4. Assess the Risks of Each Option
5. Calculate the Decision Factors
6. Make and Implement Your Decision

So what then constitutes a good choice or decision? Being able to make a good decision really depends on how well you have prepared yourself to make it. There are five important elements in a good decision. First, you must have come to the realization that there is a choice to be made. That may sound apparent and obvious to you, but in reality, it isn't always evident. Second, you need to state the purpose or intention for your decision, or why this decision is considered important to you and your organization. Third, you must fully and completely define the factors or criteria that you need to satisfy in order for the decision to be considered a good one. Fourth, you have to determine what actions or options will best satisfy the factors that you think are important. Remember you will typically have multiple options to choose from. Finally, you must consider the risks and potential negative consequences associated with your choice of options. Even though an option might meet all of the criteria needed to satisfy your decision requirements, if it carries a large risk factor, then perhaps the option isn't worth the risk to you or your organization.

The important thing to keep in mind as you proceed through the decision process is that whatever your decision happens to be, you must live with the consequences. It is because of this fact that you must take your time, weigh the benefits versus the risks, only consider facts rather than emotions, and then make the right decision, one that you can live with.

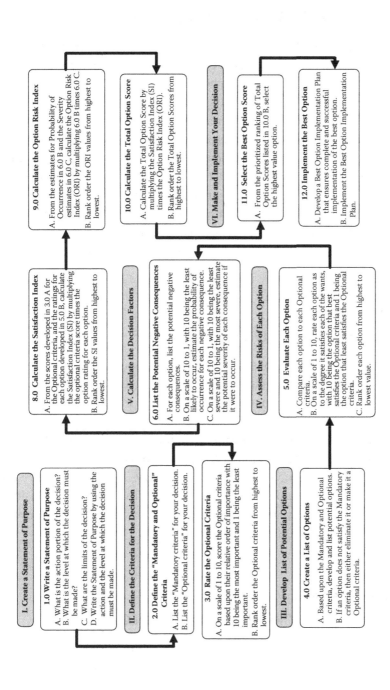

I. Create a Statement of Purpose

1.0 Write a Statement of Purpose
A. What is the action portion of the decision?
B. What is the level at which the decision must be made?
C. What are the limits of the decision?
D. Write the Statement of Purpose by using the action and the level at which the decision must be made.

II. Define the Criteria for the Decision

2.0 Define the "Mandatory and Optional" Criteria
A. List the "Mandatory criteria" for your decision.
B. List the "Optional criteria" for your decision.

3.0 Rate the Optional Criteria
A. On a scale of 1 to 10, score the Optional criteria based upon their relative order of importance with 10 being the most important and 1 being the least important.
B. Rank order the Optional criteria from highest to lowest.

III. Develop List of Potential Options

4.0 Create a List of Options
A. Based upon the Mandatory and Optional criteria, develop and list potential options.
B. If an option does not satisfy the Mandatory criteria, then either eliminate it or make it a Optional criteria.

IV. Assess the Risks of Each Option

5.0 Evaluate Each Option
A. Compare each option to each Optional criteria.
B. On a scale of 1 to 10, rate each option as to the degree it satisfies each of the wants, with 10 being the option that best satisfies the Optional criteria and 1 being the option that least satisfies the Optional criteria.
C. Rank order each option from highest to lowest value.

V. Calculate the Decision Factors

6.0 List the Potential Negative Consequences
A. For each option, list the potential negative consequences.
B. On a scale of 10 to 1, with 10 being the least likely to occur, estimate the probability of occurrence for each negative consequence.
C. On a scale of 10 to 1, with 10 being the least severe and 10 being the most severe, estimate the potential severity of each consequence if it were to occur.

8.0 Calculate the Satisfaction Index
A. From the scores developed in 3.0 A for the Optional criteria, and the ratings for each option developed in 5.0 B, calculate the Satisfaction Index (SI) by multiplying the optional criteria score times the option rating for each option.
B. Rank order the SI values from highest to lowest.

9.0 Calculate the Option Risk Index
A. From the estimates for Probability of Occurrence in 6.0 B and the Severity estimates in 6.0 C, calculate the Option Risk Index (ORI) by multiplying 6.0 B times 6.0 C.
B. Rank order the ORI values from highest to lowest.

10.0 Calculate the Total Option Score
A. Calculate the Total Option Score by multiplying the Satisfaction Index (SI) times the Option Risk Index (ORI).
B. Rank order the Total Option Scores from highest to lowest.

VI. Make and Implement Your Decision

11.0 Select the Best Option Score
A. From the prioritized ranking of Total Option Scores listed in 10.0 B, select the highest value option.

12.0 Implement the Best Option
A. Develop a Best Option Implementation Plan that ensures complete and successful implementation of the best option.
B. Implement the Best Option Implementation Plan.

FIGURE 24.1
Decision Making Roadmap.

24.2 CREATE A STATEMENT OF PURPOSE

Each decision you make must always be made with a specific purpose or intention in mind. A good statement of purpose includes an action you are going to take and the result that you hope to achieve by taking this action. The statement of purpose sets the stage for everything that follows in the decision process, so it must be comprehensive enough to provide direction and include a defined set of limits, especially if there is a team involved in making the decision. If your statement of purpose, for example, was simply to improve the shipping of product to your customers, it might provide some sense of direction, but it would hardly set any limits. A better statement of purpose, in this case, might be to improve your on-time delivery from 80% to 95% to customer X within six months or less. This statement provides a clear sense of direction and has well-defined limits.

24.3 WRITE A STATEMENT OF PURPOSE

Writing a statement of purpose involves defining four separate elements, and then combining them into a single statement. The four elements are defining the intended action, the results you hope to achieve, setting the level at which the decision is to be made, and then defining the limits of the decision. Using the earlier example, "To improve our on-time delivery from 80% to 95% to customer X within six months or less," we see that the intended *action* is improving on-time delivery. The *result* we hope to achieve is to increase the on-time delivery to 95%. The *level* of the decision is that we want to achieve this improvement for customer X, and the *limit* we have set is to do so in six months or less.

24.4 DEFINE THE CRITERIA FOR THE DECISION

There are two types of criteria that are involved in all decisions. First, there are things we must have, or that are *mandatory,* in order to guarantee that our final decision will be successful, and then there is everything else that falls into the *optional* criteria category. When we consider options later in this process that are intended to deliver our statement of purpose, an option either satisfies the mandatory criteria or it does not. If the option doesn't meet all of the mandatory criteria, then we must either eliminate it or transfer it to our list of optional criteria. All mandatory criteria must be measurable and clearly defined, with no ambiguity.

Optional criteria, on the other hand, are the things that are not mandatory, but they would be nice to have if we could get them. For example, if you were buying a car, one of your mandatory criteria might be that the price must be under $30,000, and any car that is over this price would not be considered and automatically be rejected. On the other hand, if you wanted a red car but would buy a car that was a different color, then the color red would be an optional criterion. The options that we are considering will be judged on their relative performance against the optional criteria. Remember, we are simply comparing options against each other, and optional criteria help us draw this comparison.

24.5 RATE THE OPTIONAL CRITERIA

Now that you have developed a list of optional criteria, you must now give each one of them an individual score from 1 to 10 based upon their relative order of importance to each other. First you must identify which of the optional criteria is the most important to you and rate it as a 10. All other optional criteria are then rated in comparison to this most important one. Obviously, then, a rating of 10 is the most important, while a rating of 1 is the least important. Keep in mind that there could be more than one of the optional criteria rated as a 10, but you must be totally honest and objective when rating these types of criteria. When this step is completed, rank order them from the highest to the smallest rating. We do this to give a visual display of all of the criteria compared to each other. So if the final ordering of these criteria appear to be out of order in some way, now is the time to discuss and reorder them if necessary.

24.6 DEVELOP A LIST OF POTENTIAL OPTIONS THAT SATISFY THE DECISION CRITERIA

The ultimate option would be one that satisfies all the mandatory and optional criteria, but, unfortunately, these kinds of options are few and far between, so we use our evaluative skills to make an informed decision. In some cases, there may only be one option to consider, so our decision in this case is whether or not the results it is intended to deliver are adequate enough to meet our needs. It is important to remember that the way we are currently doing things should always be considered as an option, even though we aren't happy with the results.

24.7 EVALUATE AND RATE EACH OPTION

Now that we have a list of potential options, we now need to compare each option as to how it satisfies the mandatory and optional criteria. For the mandatory criteria, the option either satisfies it or it doesn't. If it doesn't, then eliminate it immediately. For the optional criteria, we need to compare each option to each of the optional criteria and give it a rating of 1 to 10, with 10 meaning that the option satisfies the optional criterion totally and 1 meaning that it in no way satisfies it. When you have finished scoring the options, rank order the options from the highest score to the lowest to give a visual comparison of all options. By rating each option against its ability to satisfy the mandatory and optional criteria, we are evaluating the option's quality of fit.

24.8 ASSESS THE RISKS OF EACH OPTION

Just like we did in the Problem Prevention Roadmap, we now need to assess the risks, or potential negative consequences, of each option. We do this in two ways. First, we need to brainstorm, discuss, and list any potential negative consequences associated with each option. Once this is completed to our satisfaction, we then must estimate the probability that each of these potential negative consequences might occur. Here we need to rely on things like our past experiences in a similar situation, research information, and our own intuition. Again, we apply a rating of 10 to 1, with 1 in this case meaning that the consequence is likely to occur and 10 meaning that it will probably not occur. In this case, we are not rating one consequence against the others but rather each one individually.

Not only are we concerned about whether a negative consequence will occur, we are also interested in the impact or severity on the organization if it does occur. Again, we use a scale of 10 to 1, with 1 interpreted as being catastrophic to the organization and 10 meaning there will be little or no impact on the organization if the consequence were to occur. The numbers between 10 and 1 are indicative of increasing or decreasing severity on the organization. When you complete this rating, once again arrange the consequences from highest to lowest based upon their individual ratings.

24.9 CALCULATE THE SATISFACTION INDEX

Now that we have completed the hard work of assigning rankings to the optional criteria and the options, it is now time to make a preliminary calculation referred to as the Satisfaction Index. This index is a measure of how well each option stacks up against each optional criterion. This is done by multiplying the optional criteria score we assigned in section 3.0A of the Decision Making Roadmap times the rating we have given for each option that we assigned in 5.0B of the roadmap. The formula for the Satisfaction Index (SI) is

$$SI = \text{Optional criteria score} \times \text{Option score}$$

For example, suppose we rated an optional criterion as a 9 and an option as a 6, then the Satisfaction Index for this criterion and option would be

$$SI = 9 \times 6 = 54$$

Pretty straightforward, isn't it? Once you have completed the math for all options and all optional criteria, arrange them in numerical order from highest to lowest. The results you get may surprise you.

24.10 CALCULATE THE OPTION RISK INDEX

Now it is time to assess the risk associated with each individual option. Even though an option might have scored the highest for the Satisfaction Index, doesn't guarantee that it will be your final selection. It is now time to calculate the Option Risk Index (ORI). This is done by multiplying the estimate for probability of occurrence from 6.0B in the roadmap for each option times the corresponding severity estimates you assigned earlier. The formula for the Option Risk Index is

$$\text{ORI} = \text{Probability of occurence rating (O)} \times \text{Severity rating (S)}$$

or

$$\text{ORI} = \text{O} \times \text{S}$$

Suppose we had rated occurrence for an option as 8 and severity as a 9, then the ORI would be equal to $9 \times 8 = 72$.

Once the Option Risk Index has been calculated for each option being considered, rank order the ORI values from highest to lowest. Does the order of the ORI look the same as the SI list? If it doesn't, then the risks may dictate a new best option.

24.11 CALCULATE THE TOTAL OPTION SCORE

Now that we have calculated the Satisfaction Index and the Option Risk Index, it is now time to calculate one more number, the Total Option Score (TOS). The Total Option Score will be used to separate all of the available options from best to worst and set the stage for your decision. The Total Option Score is calculated by multiplying the Satisfaction Index times the Option Risk Index as follows:

$$\text{Total Option Score (TOS)} = \text{Satisfaction Index (SI)} \times \text{Option Risk Index (ORI)}$$

or

$$\text{TOS} = \text{SI} \times \text{ORI}$$

Suppose we had calculated the SI to be 54 and the ORI to be 72, then the TOS would be

$$TOS = 54 \times 72 = 3888$$

Calculate the Total Option Score for each of the options, and then rank order them from highest to lowest.

24.12 MAKE YOUR DECISION

From the prioritized rankings for the Total Option Scores, select the TOS at the top of the list. If you have done everything correctly and not interjected emotion into the scoring or rankings for each option and each optional criteria, then the TOS with the highest score should be your best option for your decision. Most of the time, if you have done everything according to the Decision Making Roadmap, your decision-making prowess should improve dramatically.

24.13 IMPLEMENT THE BEST OPTION

Just like any implementation, you should think about it and create a plan that ensures the complete and successful implementation of the best option. The best option implementation plan must include a detailed list of items that must be done, as well as the order in which they are to be completed. I have seen several good decisions made that were implemented without thought, and the results were disastrous. Take your time like you would any other implementation.

25

A Case Study in Decision Making

A real decision is measured by the fact that you've taken a new action. If there's no action, you haven't truly decided.

Anthony Robbins

25.1 CASE BACKGROUND

You will recall the high-speed bottling company in Chapter 23 that conducted a problem prevention exercise involving a potential shortage of oil-based resin. The company had identified several potential problems with its resin supplier and had put plans in place to reduce the likelihood of a shortage. The plans were primarily concerned with the resin supplier implementing effective safety and preventive maintenance programs. The bottling company had informed the supplier that if it didn't comply with both of these initiatives that it would source a new supplier. Things worked well for a period of time, but it wasn't long before shortages started occurring. The leadership team had decided to go ahead with its plan to source and certify a new resin supplier.

The bottling company called me in to help with the selection, but I explained that the only thing I could do for them was help make their decision as to which supplier would be the best option. The CEO agreed and called his team together for a meeting. I asked them what they had done so far in their search for this new resin supplier, and, not surprisingly, all they had done was bicker over who the supplier should be. There had been no structured attempt to develop a statement of purpose or even define any criteria for the selection of the new resin supplier.

As with the problem prevention exercise, I explained to them that there was a best way of approaching a decision like this and, like the problem prevention exercise, there was a roadmap to follow. Since the team members had enjoyed a positive experience before, they were eager to hear what I had to say. The first thing I did was hand out a copy of the Decision Making Roadmap.

Figure 25.1 is the twelve-step procedure that I introduced in Chapter 24, so the first order of business was to explain how it was to be used. We started by focusing on creating a statement of purpose. I explained that a good statement of purpose includes an action you are going to take and the result that you hope to achieve by taking this action. I told them that the statement of purpose sets the stage for everything that follows in the decision process, so it must be comprehensive enough to provide direction and include a defined set of limits, especially if there is a team involved in making the decision. The team brainstormed and came up with the following statement: "Find a resin supplier that can deliver a non-oil-based resin to replace our current oil-based resin made to our specifications and price within five months."

The statement included the action the team wanted to take, the results it wanted to achieve, and the limits under which the decision would be made. Armed with a good statement of purpose, it was time to define the criteria under which the decision would be judged.

25.2 DEFINE THE CRITERIA FOR THE DECISION

I explained to the team that there are two types of criteria that are involved in all decisions. First, there are requirements we must have or that are *mandatory* in order to guarantee that our final decision will be successful, and then there is everything else that falls into the *optional* criteria category. Optional criteria are the things that are not mandatory, but they would be nice to have if we could get them. I explained that the options that we would be considering later will be judged on their relative performance against the optional criteria.

Having explained the difference between the mandatory criteria and optional criteria, we began our definition exercise. The team brainstormed and developed a great list of mandatory criteria. Its list included

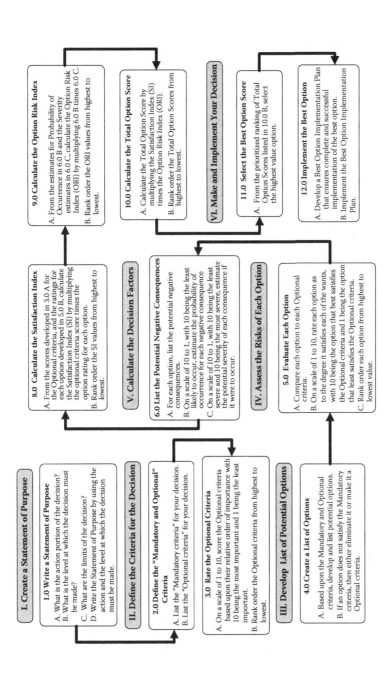

FIGURE 25.1

Decision Making Roadmap.

measurable criteria for cost, production capacity, preventive maintenance, safety, and on-time delivery rates as follows:

1. Cost per pound must be less than or equal to X.
2. Must prove their production capacity for the new resin to be greater than or equal to X pounds per year.
3. Preventive maintenance plan in place, on schedule, and unplanned downtime less than or equal to X.
4. Vigorous safety program in place, with accident rates less than or equal to X.
5. Proof of on-time delivery rate to all customers greater than or equal to X.
6. Demonstrated quality levels must be less than or equal to X parts per million.

The team next brainstormed and developed a list of optional criteria as follows:

1. Within 500 miles of our production facility
2. ISO 9000 certified
3. Six Sigma program in place
4. Able to deliver resin by rail
5. Active R&D program, with a history of new product introductions
6. Demonstrated Lean manufacturing principles

Once again, the team had compiled a very good list of optional criteria and was now ready for the next step in the process.

25.3 RATE THE OPTIONAL CRITERIA

With the list of optional criteria in place, it was now time for the team to select the most important optional criterion, rate it as a 10, and then rate the remaining optional criteria from 1 to 10 relative to the most important optional criterion. The team did so as demonstrated in Table 25.1. This was an unusual exercise for me, in that normally the optional criteria outnumber the mandatory criteria.

TABLE 25.1

Optional Criteria

Optional Criteria	Rating
1. Within 500 miles of our production facility	10
2. Active R&D program with a history of new product introductions	8
3. Able to deliver resin by rail	7
4. Demonstrated Lean manufacturing principles	5
5. ISO 9000 certified	2
6. Six Sigma program in place	1

25.4 DEVELOP A LIST OF POTENTIAL OPTIONS

Now that the team had its mandatory and important optional criteria in place, and had rated and ranked them, it was now time to begin the job of creating potential options that will meet the team's needs and permit it to make an informed decision. In this particular decision-making process, we were comparing resin manufacturers and ranking them against their ability to meet the mandatory and optional criteria.

The team spent the next week researching resin manufacturers through industry publications, making telephone calls to friends in the industry, and searching on the Internet. The team selected four resin manufacturers and was ready to continue the decision-making process.

25.5 EVALUATE EACH OPTION

Now that the team had its final list of four options in place, it was time to evaluate each manufacturer for its ability to satisfy the optional criteria the team had developed. As the team developed its list of options, it automatically rejected any option that did not conform to its list of mandatory criteria. There were initially six candidates, but two were eliminated for failure to meet the mandatory criteria. One was rejected for failure to meet the cost per pound criteria, and the other had on-time delivery issues.

From Table 25.2, if the decision were only made on the basis of compliance to criteria alone, it appears as though Company D would be the team's choice. But as we learned in the last chapter, making a selection at this stage solely on the basis of compliance to criteria can prove to be

TABLE 25.2

Optional Criteria Matrix With Scores

	Option			
Optional Criteria	Company A Score	Company B Score	Company C Score	Company D Score
Within 500 miles of our production facility	9	6	5	7
Active R&D program with a history of new product introductions	3	6	9	9
Able to deliver resin by rail	1	8	7	9
Demonstrated Lean manufacturing principles	9	8	8	9
ISO 9000 certified	10	10	10	10
Six Sigma program in place	1	10	5	10

dangerous and risky. It is important to keep personal feelings and biases out of the decision-making process, so that a fair and balanced assessment can be made. It was clear that the purchasing manager had strong feelings about one of the resin companies being considered, but he was convinced by the other team members to continue with the process before a final decision was made.

25.6 ASSESS THE RISKS OF EACH OPTION

Once again, the team researched each resin manufacturer to define and evaluate any potential negative consequences or risks associated with each company. The team spent two weeks on this activity and discovered some legitimate risks related to each potential choice as a new resin supplier. Some were rumors and some were facts, so investigating each company in depth would be critical to the success of the team's decision.

Table 25.3 is a summary of the potential negative consequences that the team came up with for each of the four options it was considering. Some were rumors that had to be investigated, while others were factual and published within the company's 10K documentation. The team now has all of the information it needs to make a decision on which option to choose.

TABLE 25.3

Matrix of Potential Negative Consequences

Potential Negative Consequence	Company A		Company B		Company C		Company D	
	O	S	O	S	O	S	O	S
Rumor of a potential strike by the union could cause a long-term interruption of resin.	5	3						
Historical PPM quality levels were greater than *X* that could return.			6	3				
Rumor that the company will be sold to competitor, which could negate any long-term contracts.					4	4		
Safety record in past was not acceptable, which could interrupt our supply of resin.							6	6
CEO announced his retirement within a year and new CEO could change the direction of the company.	1	2						
Quality manager resigned last month, which could negatively impact quality of incoming resin.					1	3		
Three years ago, company had an explosion that shut down its resin reactor. If it were to happen again, resin supply could be in jeopardy.			4	7				

25.7 CALCULATE THE DECISION FACTORS

The team is getting closer to making a final decision, but before it does there are several calculations that must be made. The data that has been collected thus far will be used to analyze each company from two perspectives. First, how well does each option satisfy each of the individual optional criteria? The second calculation considers the potential risks and negative consequences that each option might bring.

25.8 CALCULATE THE SATISFACTION INDEX

So far, the team has rated each of the optional criteria in terms of their relative importance. The team did this by determining the most important optional criterion rating it as a 10, and then rated each of the other ones relative to the most important criterion. Next, the team rated each option for how well it satisfied each of the individual optional criteria. It is now time to put both of these ratings together to form a Satisfaction Index (SI). The SI is calculated by multiplying each criterion times the rating the team placed on each option. The team will then add the total multiple scores together to arrive at a Satisfaction Index, as seen in Table 25.4.

Based upon the Satisfaction Index, the order of choice of the final option would have been

1. Company D: 290 points
2. Company C: 248 points
3. Company B: 244 points
4. Company A: 188 points

As stated earlier, if we were to end our decision process after we calculated the Satisfaction Index, then Company D would be the clear choice.

25.9 CALCULATE THE OPTION RISK INDEX

Each option being considered for selection carries with it a risk or a potential negative consequence. Earlier the team had estimated the probability of occurrence and potential severity associated with each potential negative consequence. It is now time to calculate the Option Risk Index (ORI) by multiplying the probability of occurrence rating (O) times the severity rating (S) that the team developed earlier. In this case, the higher the number, the more favorably the team will look on the option. Table 25.5 is a summary of these ratings. Since company B has the highest ORI value, if the team was considering only this index, it would probably have selected this option. But we have one more score to calculate.

TABLE 25.4

Completed Matrix of Optional Criteria and Ranking by Company

Optional Criteria	Optional Criteria Ranking	Option							
		Company A		Company B		Company C		Company D	
		Score	Total	Score	Total	Score	Total	Score	Total
Within 500 miles of our production facility	10	9	90	6	60	5	50	7	70
Active R&D program with a history of new product introductions	8	3	24	6	48	9	72	9	72
Able to deliver resin by rail	7	1	7	8	56	7	56	9	63
Demonstrated Lean manufacturing principles	5	9	45	8	40	8	40	9	45
ISO 9000 certified	2	10	20	10	20	10	20	10	20
Six Sigma program in place	2	1	2	10	20	5	10	10	20
Total	N/A		188		244		248		290

TABLE 25.5

Potential Negative Consequences by Company

Potential Negative Consequence	Company A			Company B			Company C			Company D		
	O	S	ORI	O	S	ORI	O	S	ORI	O	S	ORI
Rumor of a potential strike by the union could cause a long-term interruption of resin.	5	3	15									
Historical PPM quality levels were greater than X that could return.				6	3	18						
Rumor that the company will be sold to competitor, which could negate any long-term contracts.							4	4	16			
Safety record in past was not acceptable, which could interrupt our supply of resin.										6	6	36
CEO announced his retirement within a year and new CEO could change the direction of the company.	1	2	2									
Quality manager resigned last month, which could negatively impact quality of incoming resin.							1	3	3			
Three years ago, company had an explosion that shut down its resin reactor. If it were to happen again, resin supply could be in jeopardy.				4	7	28						
Total			17			46			19			36

TABLE 25.6

Total Option Score

Option	Satisfaction Index	Option Risk Index	Total Option Score
Company A	188	17	3196
Company B	244	46	11224
Company C	248	19	4712
Company D	290	36	10440

25.10 CALCULATE THE TOTAL OPTION SCORE

It was now time for the team to calculate the Total Option Score for each of the options. The Total Option Score is an amalgam or mixture of how the team rated the optional criteria, how the team felt each option stacked up against each criterion, and the risks associated with each of the options. Table 25.6 is a summary of the Total Option Score for each of the options.

So based upon the calculation of the Total Option Score, company B is the highest rated supplier of the four that were investigated and scrutinized. Looking at the four options more closely, however, we see that the top two options really are quite close to each other in scoring. Remember a scoring difference of one or two points, prior to multiplication, can translate into a significant difference after multiplication is complete. When Total Option Scores are close like this, it is really a matter of which option you feel more comfortable with.

25.11 MAKE AND IMPLEMENT YOUR DECISION

Now that all of the data gathering, risk assessments, ratings, rankings, and calculations have been completed, it was now time for the team to make its final decision. The team discussed both of the two highest scoring options, and decided to select company D rather than company B for two primary reasons as follows:

1. Company D had the fewest number of negative consequences.
2. Company D had the highest satisfaction index, which was indicative of how well it would most likely satisfy the optional criteria.

The team was also more impressed with how quickly company D responded to all of its requests. Intuition, although not data-based, is certainly an important part of any decision and, as a team, the team felt good about its final decision. Either option would have been acceptable, so I supported the team's decision.

25.12 IMPLEMENT THE BEST OPTION

Just like any implementation, the certification and use of a new supplier must be done so deliberately and with a well-conceived action plan. For this reason, the team developed a very comprehensive *best option implementation plan*. The plan was jointly developed with the new supplier and included things like the creation of a safety stock to guard against any negative response by the current supplier. The plan also called for prototype studies to ensure that the new supplier's product produced bottles that would conform to the bottle company's specifications. As it turned out, company D had a well-defined prototype process of its own, and the transition to the new product was virtually seamless.

26

Needs Assessment

Yesterday is the best way to work tomorrow.

Jon Madonna

26.1 PUTTING IT ALL TOGETHER

So far, you have learned about preventing and solving problems, as well as making decisions. I have given you roadmaps to follow for each of the three actions that you or your organization will be faced with as you do your jobs. When or where to use each of these roadmaps will be obvious to most of you, but for some, it won't be. It is for these people that I end this book with this chapter on assessment of needs.

But before I talk about assessing your needs, I want everyone to understand the intentions of the roadmaps. Think about what you do before you leave for a new destination in your car. Most people do one of two things. Either they log onto MapQuest, use their GPS, or some other Internet location finder to get specific directions (and a simple map), or they buy a map or an atlas and map out their own set of directions. If this location is one that you will be visiting frequently, then after several trips you will no longer need the GPS, maps, or directions, because you just know the way. So too is the intention of the roadmaps presented in this book. Use them and learn them, and they will become committed to memory. The old adage of practice makes perfect is really true. The point is, as you become familiar and comfortable with each of the three roadmaps, you will no longer need them, because you will know exactly what to do next. You will have put it all together, and it will eventually become a habit.

As you continue using the roadmaps, you will soon learn that you will no longer need to follow each of the individual steps in a logical and regimented way. They will become instinctive and automatic to you as you work through existing problems, prevent future problems, or make decisions and choices about different options you have.

26.2 ASSESSING YOUR NEEDS

As I indicated earlier, some of you will automatically understand when to use each of the three roadmaps, but others will not. For all of you I have developed a *Needs Assessment Roadmap* as shown in Figure 26.1.

The Needs Assessment Roadmap is really a series of questions that you must answer as the circumstance you are faced with presents itself. The first two questions you must answer are, Is there a problem to be solved? followed by the question, Does the problem already exist? If the problem already exists, then you can proceed immediately to the Problem Solving Roadmap. Once there, you will be able to guide yourself through the steps until you have reached the root cause of the problem. Once you have the root cause, you will then be guided through developing a solution to the problem.

If the answer to the second question is no, then you must answer this question: Is there a problem to be prevented? Since this indicates that you are contemplating that a problem could arise, then you will proceed to the Problem Prevention Roadmap. Once there, you will follow the steps to identify the high-risk areas, the potential failure modes and effects, and the potential root cause, followed by the development and implementation of a preventive measures plan.

The next question is, Is there a decision involved? If the decision has already been made, then it is a good idea to follow the Problem Prevention Roadmap to be certain that you have considered all of the potential problems and risks relative to your decision. If the decision has not been made, then you can proceed to the Decision Making Roadmap. There you will be guided through all of the steps to, first, develop a statement of purpose that includes the reason for the decision, the actions to be taken, and the level and limits of the decision. You will then develop the mandatory and

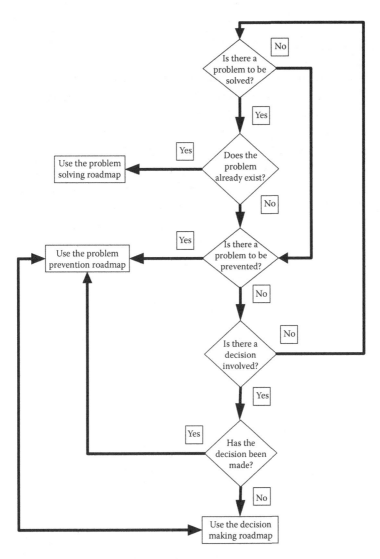

FIGURE 26.1
Needs Assessment Roadmap.

optional criteria to be satisfied by the decision, develop options, assess the risks, and then select the best options.

I am hopeful that the Needs Assessment Roadmap will help those of you who are having difficulty deciding which of the roadmaps to follow. I think I have kept it simple and straightforward for you.

26.3 CONCLUSION

We are all confronted with decisions and problems every day, but most certainly in our work life, knowing what to do can sometimes be filled with pressure and uncertainty. It is my hope that the roadmaps that I have developed will help guide you through the sometimes overpowering and overwhelming inventory of problems and decisions that we all face on a routine basis. The common thread that binds all of these roadmaps is the essential yet fundamental need to follow a structured and systematic process. I hope I have helped to provide a coherent and effective pathway. I wish you good luck, but as I told you in the Preface, my definition of luck is *l*aboring *u*nder *c*orrect *k*nowledge. You make your own luck!

Appendix: Problem Analysis Flowchart

Process:
Date:

Problem statement — 1.

What?

Where?

When?

Scope?

Trend?

Statement:

Symptoms — 2.

1.
2.
3.

Relevant data — 3.

1.

2.

3.

Potential Causes

⟶ Causal chain

Conclusions

Results

When made

Tests/corrections

Changes

1.
2.
3.
4. — 4.

Defect free configuration

1.
2.
3.
4. — 5.

Distinctions

1.

2.

3. — 6.

Tests/corrections

1.
2.
3.
4.
5.
6.
7.

Problem statement

What? 1.

Where? 2.

When? 3.

Scope? 4.

Trend? 5.

Statement: 6.

1.

Changes

1.
2.
3.
4.
5.
6.

4.

Most probable cause(s) and comments

1.
2.
3.
4.
5.

Corrections/controls

Short term

Corrections:

Controls:

Long term

Corrections:

Controls

9.

Symptoms

1.
2.
3.
4.

2.

Defect free config's

1.
2.
3.
4.

5.

Relevant data

1.

2.

3.

3.

Distinctions

1.
2.
3.
4.

6.

Tests/corrections

1.
2.
3.
4.
5.
6.

When made

Results

Conclusions

10.

References

1. Charles Kepner and Benjamin Tregoe, *The Rational Manager: A Systematic Approach to Problem Solving and Decision-Making*, McGraw-Hill, 2006.
2. Bob Sproull, *Process Problem Solving: A Guide for Maintenance and Operations Teams*, Productivity Press, 2001.
3. Jeffrey Liker, *The Toyota Way: 14 Management Principles from the World's Greatest Manufacturer*, McGraw-Hill, 2004.
4. Roger Bohn, "Stop Fighting Fires," *Harvard Business Review*, July–August 2000.

Index

Page numbers followed by f and t indicate figures and tables, respectively.

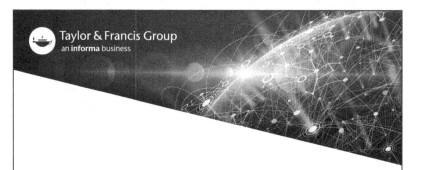

Printed in the United States
by Baker & Taylor Publisher Services